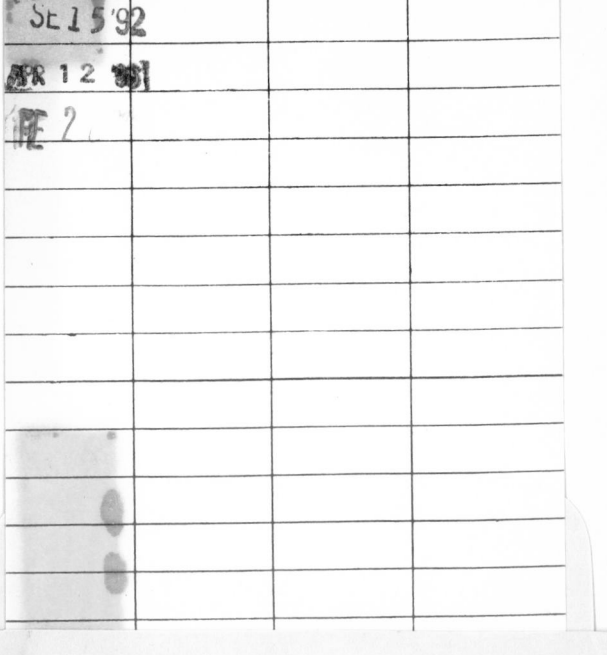

RED REVOLUTIONARY

JOAN CHARNOCK

RED REVOLUTIONARY
A Life of Lenin

★

HAWTHORN BOOKS, INC.   *Publishers*
New York

CONTENTS

RED REVOLUTIONARY

1

A Childhood in Czarist Russia

★

I t was on April 22, 1870, that Maria Alexandrovna, the
wife of Ilya Nikolayevich, gave birth to her third child, a
boy, in a large wooden house in Simbirsk (now called
Ulyanov, in Lenin's honor), a pleasant town on the great
Volga River almost in the heart of Russia.

The baby was christened Vladimir, and his full name
was Vladimir Ilyich Ulyanov. Ilyich meant "son of Ilya."
Ulyanov was his father's family name, probably derived from
the Russian word for beehive, *ulei*. Vladimir's real names,
however, have now almost been forgotten—for he is known
all over the world as Lenin, one of the many pseudonyms he
adopted in the course of his career, and the one he retained
to the end of his life.

Lenin's father had quite a good position as a school inspector. There was Tartar blood in the family, and Lenin himself was slightly Asiatic in appearance.

Ilya, Lenin's father, owed a great deal to his elder brother, Vasily. Their father, a tailor, had died in 1838 when Ilya was only seven years old, leaving the family practically penniless. Vasily, who was sixteen, gave up his own ambition to go to a university, and instead started work in an office to support the family. He was very anxious for his brother, Ilya, to have the university education he had missed himself. Fortunately, Ilya was quite good at mathematics, and when he was only fourteen he gave lessons to other students. Eventually, in 1850, he managed to get a scholarship to the University of Kazan, where he was lucky to study under one of the most famous of Russian scientists, Professor Lobachevsky, who invented non-Euclidean geometry.

Ilya seems to have been a perfect student. He did very well in his work; there is no record of his ever having been in any trouble, and after he left the university he got two posts which he was able to hold simultaneously—he taught mathematics at a school for noblemen's daughters at the town of Penza, south of Kazan, and he also directed the meteorological station there.

Among his colleagues at the school was a Professor Veretennikov, who made friends with Ilya and decided that this intelligent and kind young man would make an excellent husband for his sister-in-law, Maria Blank, one of the five daughters of a doctor with a country estate. Ilya had by then taught for some years and was thirty-two. Maria, who was twenty-six, fell deeply in love with him and the marriage was a great success. They had seven children, of whom six grew up: Anna, Alexander, Vladimir (Lenin), Olga, Dmitri, and Maria.

Maria, Lenin's mother whose family was German in origin, had been brought up rather conventionally in a well-to-do country home, and now she and her husband Ilya carried on the traditions of comfort and quiet, unexciting pleasures in their married life.

They came to Simbirsk with their two elder children a few months before Lenin was born, and found it an attractive place, especially in spring and early summer, when the orchards surrounding it were in blossom and full of singing nightingales.

Although Lenin's mother had a big family, she had a fair amount of spare time because, as was usual in Russian homes in those days, many servants were kept. During the summer, Maria Alexandrovna, as she was called because her father's Christian name was Alexander, did a great deal of gardening. She loved to grow flowers and trees. Because the summers were very dry there was much watering to be done, and all the children who were old enough to carry cans of water had to run to and fro on summer evenings watering the garden.

Ilya, her husband, was not so fond of gardening, but he liked to eat the fruit the garden produced and to play croquet on the lawn.

Maria Alexandrovna taught herself French and English; she was musical, and the family were encouraged to play the piano and sing. They produced a weekly newspaper for themselves called *The Sabbath*.

In the summer there was plenty to do in Simbirsk: swimming, boating, and—what Lenin particularly enjoyed—look-

In a country the size of Russia, local government of an effective kind would be important even under modern conditions. Before the time of cars, airplanes, radio, and television, people who lived far from the capital could be cut off for months at a time in winter.

The Zemtvos were an attempt, among other things, to improve medical services and education in the provincial districts of Russia. Quite a number of young men and women who belonged to comfortably-off families worked in the Zemtvos because they were eager to help the peasants.

Besides these unselfish people, who set to work to do something practical to improve the lot of the villagers, an increasing number of men and women believed that revolution was the only way to remedy social injustice, and were prepared to spend all their time working for this end.

These revolutionaries were to be found more than anywhere else at the universities. Many of the students were very poor—just as Lenin's father had been—and were only able to come to the university because of scholarships. Whereas Lenin's father had concentrated upon his work and, after passing his examinations, took posts away from the university, there were many students who, once in the university, wanted to stay there as long as possible. Some of them spent more time planning revolution than they did studying. Their ideas included use of violent methods, such as killing important people by throwing bombs.

Russia had no parliament. The Czar was an absolute ruler. He had advisers around him, but these were not chosen by the country but by the Czar himself, and if he did not like one of them, he could dismiss him.

Everything depended upon what the Czar's own views were, and nothing could be published that the Czar and his advisers did not like. In fact, the censorship on what was printed was not as severe as it became after the Revolution, but there were secret police on the look-out for revolutionaries, and those who got into trouble were generally sent away to live in Siberia.

Russia was not then a highly industrialized country. By far the greater number of peasants lived in villages and worked on the land, and of those who worked in factories some only did so in the winter months.

Several of the chief industries in Russia were run largely by foreigners, especially English and Scottish people who managed factories and were usually very successful at getting along with the Russians.

When Lenin was born the Czar was Alexander II. He was not only a kindly man but one with quite advanced views. He had already freed the serfs. He was very much influenced by a man who had been one of his tutors when he was a boy, Vasily Andreyevich Zhukovsky. The illegitimate child of a Russian father and a Turkish mother, Zhukovsky was a poet, and he also translated English and French poetry, including Gray's *Elegy*, into Russian.

Although Zhukovsky spent much of his life as a courtier, and was very successful in getting a good position for himself, he was also deeply moved with pity for the serfs. He had given freedom to his own before the law was passed which made it compulsory to do so, and had spent some of his own money on buying other people's serfs to set them free. His influence upon the Czar was a good one. After establishing the Zemtvos, Alexander went on to reform the Courts of Justice, so that there should be equal laws for all and less bribery.

It looked as if Russia was in a happier state than ever

before, but this was all changed in 1881, when Lenin was eleven. On March 13 a tragedy occurred, terrible in itself and even more terrible in its consequences.

Czar Alexander had known for years that his life was constantly in danger from violent revolutionaries. As there was no parliament, he represented to the people their government, but, in spite of all that he had done to bring about reforms, a not very successful war with Turkey had made him unpopular.

Refusing to look after his own safety, he continued to make public appearances. Several attempts on his life had failed, but on March 13 when he was driving through the heart of St. Petersburg a bomb was thrown at his carriage. He was not hurt, but his Cossack guards were, and he got out of his carriage to speak to them. A second bomb was thrown. Fatally injured by it, he could just ask to be taken back to his palace where he died.

This crime made the Russian Revolution almost inevitable. The authorities decided that the policy of greater freedom which had been started was wrong, and they tried to suppress all more advanced ideas by harshness. Any revolutionary activity was severely punished. The new Czar, Alexander III, quite unlike his father, held to the policy of making no concessions at all.

2

An Early Tragedy

★

U ntil Lenin was fifteen years old, his home life was a
very pleasant one. He belonged to an affectionate,
intelligent family that had enough money to live in
comfort. His father, Ilya, had advanced from being a school
teacher to being a school inspector, and, as such, was responsible for the founding of hundreds of new schools, and considered an important person.

Ilya's wife's family owned a beautiful country estate
called Kokushkino, not far from Kazan. Every year the
Ulyanov family went there in the summer months. They
traveled as far as Kazan by steamer on the Volga, and then
went on to the estate which overlooked the River Ushna.
They spent much time boating and swimming, and some-

times hunted in the surrounding woods where wolves howled and occasionally a great brown bear lumbered along or a giant elk appeared.

Lenin loved this summer home. He remembered all his life how he searched the birch and pine woods for mushrooms of different kinds, while his mother worked in the flower garden. Sitting on the veranda, he read poetry and novels by the great Russian writers. He was particularly fond of Pushkin and Turgenev.

It was in 1885 that a great disappointment came to his father, Ilya. He had completed twenty-five years' work as a civil servant in the Ministry of Education, but he hoped to be retained for a few more years. For some reason, however, this did not happen, and he was told he would be pensioned off in the following year. The idea of this retirement, coming before he had expected it, broke his heart and was probably one reason for his sudden death, after an illness of only a day or two, in January, 1886.

Alexander, his eldest son, was the only one of the family not at home at the time. He was a student of biology at St. Petersburg University. Unlike his father, Alexander did not have to rely upon a scholarship to enable him to go to the university. He insisted, however, upon living as a poor student, and, to his father's annoyance, had returned quite a large part of the money Ilya allowed him for expenses. Since he would not come home for the Christmas holidays because of the cost, he was not with his father when he died.

Anna, the eldest daughter, was also studying at St. Petersburg, intending to be a teacher, but she had spent Christmas with the family.

Ilya's widow was not left in need of money; she received

quite a good pension. As his elder brother was away it was Lenin, not yet sixteen, who had to take on many of the duties of the head of the family. Working hard at school at the time, the extra responsibilities made him quarrelsome with the rest of the family and showed how badly he needed the discipline his father would have given him. At his age, this was not surprising. Much stranger was the way in which his father's death affected Alexander. Anna went back to St. Petersburg after the funeral, and was quite frightened by the change in her brother, who seemed nearing a mental breakdown. Hitherto, Alexander had had a character almost too good to be true. He was a very kind person whose chief interest lay in his studies.

His father's death brought out in him a hard, ruthless streak, and when he returned to St. Petersburg after the summer holidays of 1886, which he spent with his family, he joined a group of revolutionaries. Since the assassination of Czar Alexander II in 1881, the revolutionary parties had become greatly disorganized because they were so effectively hunted down by the police. Those groups which still existed had to meet in great secrecy.

Alexander did not do things by halves. Finding that his new friends had decided that the present Czar must be killed as his father had been, he accepted it as his duty to carry this out. To finance the plan, he sold a gold medal he had been awarded for a paper he wrote on biology, and himself designed and helped to make the bombs. Other conspirators managed to obtain dynamite and nitric acid; two of them were the brothers Pilsudski from Poland, one of whom, Joseph, later became dictator of Poland.

The idea was to kill the Czar on the anniversary of Alexander II's death. Before this, however, the police intercepted a letter written by one of the conspirators which showed him to be a terrorist, and he was closely watched. The police noticed young men behaving in an odd way in the street, one carrying what appeared to be a large book. They made some arrests, and inside the supposed book found a bomb.

The police then set to work to find who were the friends of the students they had arrested, and as one or two of the prisoners gave away the names of other conspirators, a very large number of people—over seventy, in fact—were soon under arrest, of whom only about twenty were detained, including Alexander and his sister Anna.

As soon as their mother heard of their arrest she made up her mind to go at once to St. Petersburg and use all the influence she had to get her children acquitted at the trial, or, if that were impossible, to have them punished as lightly as possible. She did all she could, and quite a lot of sympathy was shown toward her. She was allowed to see her son in prison, and even to attend the trial, although it was not a public one. Nothing, however, could be done for Alexander, as he was determined not to be saved.

Far from trying to deny that he was guilty, Alexander wanted to take the whole responsibility for the plot on himself, and be the only one punished. He made a long speech at his trial attempting to justify what he had done on the grounds that terror was the only way to bring about reform of social conditions.

At the end of the trial many of the accused were sent to prison. Anna was released, but five, including Alexander himself, were sentenced to death. On May 20, 1887, they were hanged.

Lenin was at this time preparing to take his final examination at school. Not allowing himself to be distracted from his work, he passed the examination very well. The headmaster of his school was the father of a man who, like Lenin, was to be prominent in the Russian Revolution: Kerensky.

Lenin's mother, Maria, felt that she did not want to stay any longer in Simbirsk, where everyone knew her to be the mother of Alexander, who had become so notorious. She sold the Simbirsk house and then, as Lenin had been accepted as a student at Kazan University, she moved to that city. When he was sixteen, Lenin—so he said of himself—became an atheist.

Unfortunately, Lenin was dismissed from the university after only a few months. He did not really deserve this dismissal. He had attended a student protest meeting held because the Ministry of Education was so anxious to put down any trace of revolutionary feeling that teachers were dismissed if they were even suspected of liberal views. Lenin was noticed at the meeting by the police, who, since he was Alexander's brother, were on the alert for anything he might do that was at all suspicious, and they arrested him and put him in prison for a few days. In fact, Lenin, during the months he was at Kazan University, was against revolution. Studying law, he thought that reform should come through legal means. The authorities made a big mistake, and one that had tremendous consequences, when they sent him away from the university.

Anna was then living at the Kokushkino estate. Lenin and his mother joined her there, and Lenin decided to carry on his studies by himself. He was a great reader, and, without fellow students to distract him, he read not only books about law, the subject he had begun to study at Kazan University, but also books by Karl Marx.

Marx, who was born in 1819, was a German Jew. After studying law at Bonn University, he spent the rest of his life helping to organize revolutionary movements and developing a new economic theory, whereby prosperity should be equally distributed over the whole population and no one should exploit the labors of another. He spent a long time in England and was financially aided by a Lancashire cotton merchant, Engels. Marx died in 1883, but his famous book, *Das Kapital*, is still looked upon as a kind of Bible by Communists.

Lenin's reading of law was successful, for, when he took the final examination to qualify him to practice as a lawyer, he came out at the top of his group.

In the meantime, two big changes had occurred in his home life. His mother bought a small country estate of her own, hoping that Lenin would be interested in managing it and settle down as a country gentleman. This estate, surrounded by woods where wild raspberries grew, was about thirty miles from the town of Samara. In the winter the family went into town, where they had an apartment, and Lenin began to take an interest in revolutionary work there.

The other event was a very sad one. Olga, Lenin's sister, a gay, attractive girl, of whom he was particularly fond, went as a student to the University of St. Petersburg and there she died of typhoid fever, four years after the death of her brother Alexander. As it happened, Lenin was in St. Petersburg at the time, taking his examinations, and he was horrified by the dirty state of the hospital his sister was in. Her death was a great loss to him, especially as his eldest sister,

Anna, married and left home during this same period. Her husband was called Mark Elisarov.

Lenin could not settle down in the country for long to practice as a lawyer and manage his mother's estate. In 1893 he went to St. Petersburg and entered a lawyer's office there. The books by Karl Marx he had read during his quiet years in the country had had a strong effect upon him. In favor of violent methods of reform, his real intention in going to St. Petersburg was to do revolutionary work. He was eager to teach the factory workers some of Marx's ideas, and already he looked forward to revolution in spite of all the suffering this would be sure to bring to Russia.

As factories were increasing rapidly in Russia at this time, large numbers of country people were coming into St. Petersburg to work in them. It was Lenin's aim to turn these workers into revolutionaries.

One day Lenin was at a party when his eye was caught by a remarkable young woman, Nadezhda Konstantina Krupskaya. She was not pretty but her face was the kind that people look at a second time. The very severe way in which she did her hair, brushed straight back from her face, showed how broad her forehead was; her full lips pouted as if she disapproved of what she saw. All the same she seemed gentler, more feminine and sympathetic than most of the other young women interested in revolution.

Many years later an English journalist spoke of Krupskaya —the name she was always known by in later life—as one of the finest people he had come across. She was two years older than Lenin.

When he talked with her, Lenin was attracted by her dignity and her thoughtfulness. She can hardly have been

taken by his appearance for, in the few years since Alexander's death, Lenin had become quite bald and, though still
only in his early twenties, his face was lined. One of the
names by which he was called was "Starik," the Russian for
"old man."

Though his looks were not particularly attractive, Krupskaya was fascinated by Lenin's talk, his forcefulness, and the
fact that he was absolutely dedicated to bringing about revolution. They began to go out together, spending hours walking and talking. Often they did not agree, for Lenin was not
interested in Krupskaya's plans for teaching people of the
working classes to read. Although he gave all his efforts to
bringing about social reform, Leinin was not really interested in the workers as people.

As he came to know Krupskaya better, he told her about
his own family and Alexander's death. She in return told him
of her father, who had been an army officer. He had been
sent to that part of Poland which then belonged to Russia,
to put down a rebellion, and he had become fond of the
Poles and sorry for them. Most Russians hated and despised
the Poles, but Krupskaya's father, who was made a military
governor of part of Poland, did his very best to help them—so
much so that he was arrested because a Russian officer
thought he was too sympathetic with them. He even spoke
Polish.

His trial dragged on for years. He was acquitted in the
end, but he died leaving his family very poor, and, from the
time she was fourteen, Krupskaya had helped to support the
family by teaching and other work. She had inherited something of her father's kindly nature, and Lenin found her a
soothing companion.

Lenin spent much of his time disguised as a workman, visiting factory workers and talking to them of revolution. He had to look like a worker himself, for if he dressed as a professional man the police, seeing him with them, would suspect him. He and his fellow revolutionaries had various codes in which they wrote to one another. As it would have been far too dangerous to meet in large numbers, they formed themselves into "cells" of six people each. These small groups met and studied Marxism. Lenin was the one person who knew who was in these various groups, and if he was arrested, Krupskaya was to take his place.

Lenin was lucky enough to have made friends with a wealthy woman called Alexandra Kalmykova, the wife of a government official. Sympathizing with the revolutionary movement, Alexandra was very interested in educating the working classes, both by lecturing to them and by providing cheap books. This she did by running a publishing business and a bookshop, and she often provided money for printing articles.

Some years earlier an elegant and aristocratic young man called Georgi Valentinovich Plekhanov had, with two other people, founded a society to arouse the Russian working class, by means of pamphlets and books, to take more interest in getting better living conditions. Plekhanov, a striking-looking person with black beard and moustache, made speeches against the government and became so aggressive that, in 1880, he and his friend Axelrod had to leave Russia.

They settled in Geneva, where Lenin met them in the spring of 1895. He had been very seriously ill with pneumonia and, when he recovered, decided to travel for a time. Because Plekhanov was the best-known living writer on social revolution, Lenin was very eager to meet him, but he did not get along with him as well as he did with Axelrod. Plekhanov thought Lenin much too violent in his ideas. Axelrod was more anxious than Plekhanov for actual revolution, but he insisted that all the left-wing parties must work together, whereas Lenin did not like the more moderate people, who called themselves Liberals.

When he left Switzerland, Lenin went to Paris, where, to his great excitement, he met the daughter and son-in-law of Karl Marx, M. and Mme. Lafargue.

He also went to Germany, and complained in his letters to his mother of his difficulties with the language, which he found harder than French.

Lenin eventually returned to Russia with books and a duplicating machine hidden in the false bottom of his trunk.

3
Life in Siberia

★

aving returned to St. Petersburg in September, 1895, Lenin took up his revolutionary work more enthusiastically than ever. He had to depend upon his mother for money, and he gave all his time to such activities as writing and distributing propaganda leaflets. He and Krupskaya planned to issue a special newspaper for people of the working classes, which would be printed by an illegal press and called *The Worker's Cause*.

Although Lenin had not gotten along very well with Plekhanov when they were together in Switzerland, he often wrote to him and to Axelrod. It would have been far too dangerous to send these letters through the mail in the ordinary way, so Lenin hid them in the bindings of books, and Plekhanov did the same with his replies.

The first issue of *The Worker's Cause* was to come out near the end of December, but just before it should have appeared the police arrested a large number of revolutionaries, including Lenin himself and the others who were specially concerned with the paper. Lenin was put in prison for a year. He took this philosophically. He was allowed to have books sent to him from libraries, and he continued to write articles and to try to smuggle them out. He sent secret messages to his friends by writing them in milk between the lines of ordinary letters. Writing in milk is invisible ordinarily, but when it is heated the letters appear in brownish yellow. Lenin would knead little pieces of bread until they became firm and smooth, and then shape them so that he could use them as "inkpots" for his milk. If any jailer visited his cell he promptly swallowed the inkpots.

Unlike many of his fellow prisoners, he kept fit by doing exercises in his cell. By means of his secret letters and writings he remained an important person in the revolutionary organization.

In February, 1897, he was sentenced to exile for three years in Siberia, under police supervision. Exile to Siberia was a very common form of punishment in Czarist Russia, and for the more fortunate it was not too bad a fate. Some places in Siberia were much pleasanter than others and, thanks to his mother's influence, Lenin was sent to one of the pleasantest. People could make use of their private means and live a more or less normal life in Siberia, as long as they did not attempt to leave the district they were in. Exiles did various kinds of work. Some of them married, had families, and made friends with one another.

The place Lenin was to live in was called Shushenskoye,

and, again thanks to his mother, Lenin was allowed to make his own arrangements for traveling there. Before Lenin set off he visited his mother in Moscow, and stayed some little time with her.

Lenin did not then know that his ultimate destination was Shushenskoye. He had been told to go to Krasnoyarsk and there wait for further instructions. As it turned out, he spent a month or two at Krasnoyarsk, and the time passed quite pleasantly. There was not only an ordinary town library, but a magnificent private one, belonging to a very rich merchant named Yudin, which Lenin was allowed to use.

It was not until May, 1897, that he left Krasnoyarsk for Shushenskoye. Here he was comfortably lodged in the house of a well-to-do peasant. While the summer lasted, Lenin enjoyed a great deal of out-of-door life: hunting, swimming, and fishing. In the course of doing this he made friends with a few of the peasants. There were hardly any well-educated people in the village. Lenin did some writing, and he tried to make himself useful by allowing the peasants to consult him about legal matters on Sundays.

When winter set in, life became monotonous. Lenin looked out from his window at endless snow, and even this was only visible for a little while each day during the very brief period in which there was any light.

Spring, when the snow at last melted and the birch trees put on their delicate green leaves, would have been exciting anyhow, but this spring brought a great change to Lenin's life. Krupskaya had also been exiled to Siberia, to a place called Ufa, but she had applied to be transferred to Shushenskoye so that she and Lenin could be married, and this request was granted. She arrived, with her mother, one evening in May. Lenin, who had been out hunting, was greeted on his return by his future mother-in-law with the remark that he had become very fat! Krupskaya's mother did not, in fact, get along well with Lenin. She was a religious woman who disapproved of her son-in-law because he was an atheist.

Krupskaya wanted to leave the peasant's house in which Lenin had stayed before she and her mother arrived. They found a small house for themselves and settled down with the dog Lenin had acquired. Krupskaya was quite good in the garden at growing vegetables, but since she was a bad cook, they were glad when a young girl came as a servant to do this for her. Krupskaya and Lenin translated *The History of Trades Unions*, by Sidney and Beatrice Webb, two famous British Socialists, into Russian.

Lenin continued to read a great deal, and wrote a book called *The Development of Capitalism in Russia*. In the winter he enjoyed skating, at which he was very good. As the months passed he became worried by the tone of some of the books and pamphlets reaching him in his exile. These suggested that the urge for revolution was dying down, and that some kind of compromise was looked for, which would avoid the bitterness and suffering of an actual revolution.

Lenin was firmly convinced that revolution was absolutely necessary. He was unable, because of his exile, to attend the first Congress of the Russian Communist party, held at Minsk in March, 1898. Attending this meeting were only ten people, one of whom was probably a spy, for as soon as it was over, eight of the ten were arrested by the police.

As his exile drew to an end, Lenin became restlessly eager to get back to active revolutionary work. Since Krupskaya's exile lasted one year longer, and he did not choose to remain in Siberia until she was free to leave with him, Lenin had to say good-bye to his wife. In any case, from the first it was not romance but rather their common interest in revolution and willingness to work for it that had drawn them together. Later on there were one or two other women in Lenin's life, at least one of whom he loved. Even she never took the place of Krupskaya, however, whose support and help he needed all his life. Of course, his marriage to her was less important to him than his revolutionary work. There were no children.

Krupskaya was utterly devoted to Lenin, and it must have been hard for her when he returned to European Russia, leaving her and her mother to go back to her former place of exile, Ufa—for she had been allowed to live at Shushenskoye only because she was Lenin's wife.

She and her mother traveled by sledge with Lenin for two hundred miles on the frozen Yenisey River to Ufa. Here Krupskaya said good-bye to her husband, who hurried on to western Russia to resume his revolutionary work.

Lenin was not allowed to live in St. Petersburg. He could go anywhere else he liked in Russia—but always under observation by the police. St. Petersburg was naturally the place he really wanted to be in, as there were many revolutionaries there whom he knew.

He settled himself in the town of Pskov, not far from St. Petersburg, where he began his task of the moment—the production of a newspaper full of revolutionary propaganda. The idea was that this paper should be printed in Switzerland. Plekhanov, who lived in Switzerland, was to be the editor. Several revolutionaries, including Martov, of whom Lenin was to see a great deal, came for a conference in Pskov to discuss the means of doing this.

4

Lenin in London

★

L enin intended to work with Plekhanov on the publication of a magazine as well as a revolutionary newspaper, but there were many problems. The two men quarrelled continually and were critical of each other's style and opinions. Lenin, with his forceful character, took over the main direction of the paper and went to live in Munich, where he was joined by Krupskaya.

The newspaper, called *Iskra*, or *The Spark*, first appeared in December, 1900. While in Munich Lenin also wrote a book setting out his ideas on revolutions. Lenin thought a revolution should be organized by a small number of full-time, dedicated, and highly trained people, who were to have complete authority. He had no use at all for the opinions of part-time helpers, or of those who were not prepared to sacrifice everything. The rank and file must simply obey orders. Lenin's plans were like those of an army general, and he had great admiration for the organizing skill of the Germans.

Lenin wanted the working class to triumph over the property-owning class, but he had no intention of giving them liberty to do what they liked when they had triumphed. They were to be better off—because the richer classes would have their property taken away from them to be distributed evenly—but under a kind of dictatorship. Lenin's writings, even at this period, sixteen years or so before he did attain the directing power in Russia, show that he was eager to have this power.

Another feature of his plans was that he wanted his trained revolutionaries to penetrate secretly into every industry and profession, even into the police and the Orthodox Church. These men were to make revolutionary propaganda among their fellow workers, in the hope of persuading some of them to support the movement. This plan has been followed by Communists, especially in factories, and is one reason why they are so much feared by non-Communist governments.

Lenin's book was published in Germany, but since the printers of his newspaper decided that it was too dangerous to continue producing it, he was obliged to find someone else to do it. Plekhanov hoped that he would return to Switzerland, but Lenin had made up his mind that he wanted to go to London and have the paper printed in England, and he insisted upon having his way.

Lenin and Krupskaya went to London in 1902. Unfortunately, they arrived in dense fog. Krupskaya was depressed.

When the fog lifted and she saw how huge London was, she was dismayed, never having seen or imagined anything like it.

Lenin, however, thought it a good place in which to work for a year or so. He applied for permission to study in the Reading Room of the British Museum, calling himself Jacob Richter. This was only one of the many names by which Lenin was known in the course of his life. He and Krupskaya rented a two-room unfurnished apartment at 30 Holford Square, paying thirty shillings a week for it. The landlady was puzzled because Krupskaya, whom she knew as Mrs. Richter, wore no wedding ring, but she liked her for being so fond of the cat in the house. Krupskaya never tired of playing with it, even teaching it to shake hands.

Lenin spent his mornings in the British Museum, and usually in the afternoon he met other revolutionaries, for there were many living in London at the time. Deciding that his English needed improving, he took lessons from a Mr. Raymond, to whom he gave Russian lessons in exchange.

An old lady in London remembers being taken to see Lenin when she was a child. He took her on his knee and talked of a great day, which he might never live to see, though she would. She, who had been brought up in a very religious home, thought he referred to the Day of Judgment. Lenin, when he realized this, was much amused.

While they were living in London, Lenin and Krupskaya had an unexpected visit from a man called Bronstein, a Russian Jew, who was an ardent revolutionary. He was to become famous later under his adopted name, Leon Trotsky. Lenin and Trotsky, destined to have a great deal to do with one another in the course of their lives, were very different in personality. Trotsky, who at that time was known among his fellow revolutionaries as "The Pen," had, like Lenin, been in prison in Russia and in exile in Siberia. He had a great deal of personal charm, and was altogether much more colorful than Lenin, who was by nature a theorist, but a theorist full of energy and drive. Trotsky's outlook was more practical than Lenin's. Both men were ruthless and liked power. Trotsky had a much more dramatic sense of his own personality than Lenin had of his. Lenin wanted power, but he did not show interest in making himself a "figurehead." In fact, few human beings have, after their death, been given such veneration as Lenin has received.

Trotsky lived for a time in London with two other Russian revolutionaries, both of whom were working with Lenin on producing the paper, *Iskra*: Vera Zasulich and Martov, who, like Trotsky, was a Jew. Martov did not find Lenin easy to work with, and after a time he went to France. Perhaps he found the life in London too bohemian and uncomfortable. Part of a house was rented to accommodate Russian revolutionaries in London for long or short periods. They had to cook for themselves, but Vera appeared to live only on tea and cigarettes.

Lenin sometimes liked to attend Socialist meetings in the East End of London. He was in secret correspondence with many revolutionaries who were still in Russia, largely about the distribution of *Iskra* and the forming of a committee to organize a party conference. He became very depressed when the letters he received from them indicated that they were not making much headway. In these letters a code was followed. The word "handkerchief" meant a passport; "barrels of beer" were shipments of the paper *Iskra*; and "warm fur" was illegal literature. Most of the revolutionaries used false names. Krupskaya's was the Russian word for lamprey: *Mynoga*.

After Lenin and Krupskaya had lived in London for about a year, the committee that controlled *Iskra* decided that it should not be printed in London, but in Switzerland, where half the people who controlled it lived. The reasoning was that it would be better if most of the people working on the paper were in the same place. There was also a small secret printing press at Baku in the Caucasus. If many copies of *Iskra* were lost or destroyed on the way to Russia, this printing press could reproduce from any that arrived.

Smuggling the paper into Russia was one of the main tasks of the revolutionaries. In many European cities there existed groups of people who collected funds and helped the movement generally.

Lenin was unhappy at the decision to produce *Iskra* in Switzerland. He had been glad to be in London, well away from Plekhanov, with whose views he was always disagreeing. So upset was he at the idea of going back to Switzerland that he became ill, but he and Krupskaya found a lodging in a place near Geneva, where they were later joined by Krupskaya's mother. Lenin's mother and sister Anna had joined him for a vacation in France in the course of his London year.

Not long after Lenin and Krupskaya left London, the second Congress of the Communist or Socialist Democratic party took place—the first at which Lenin was able to be present. This was in 1903.

The purpose of the Congress was to make plans to carry out reforms by revolution or other means. In fact, it turned into violent quarreling between those members who agreed with Lenin, and especially with his view that only a small number of completely dedicated people should make plans, and those, including Plekhanov, who were willing to draw in sympathizers on a much wider basis. In the end the quarrel became so bitter that the Communists split into two parties, one following Lenin and the other Plekhanov.

Because more people joined Lenin than Plekhanov, Lenin's party was called the Bolshevik party, from the Russian word "Bolshoi," which means big. The other party was called the Menshevik party, from the Russian word "Menshie," meaning less. The Mensheviks, unlike the Bolsheviks, wanted reform rather than revolution. In Russia their supporters were drawn largely from the more intelligent of the working class; the less intelligent were apt to follow the Bolsheviks.

This quarrel and splitting up into two parties meant that Lenin was now dissociated not merely from Plekhanov, with whom he had long disagreed, but also from his former friends and co-workers on *Iskra*—Vera Zasulich, Martov, and Trotsky, who all decided to work with the Mensheviks.

The fact that so many prominent revolutionaries joined the Mensheviks made Lenin outstanding among the Bolsheviks.

He had taken a very aggressive line at the Congress, but the effect of what he did was to make him feel tired, ill, and discouraged. He gave up *Iskra*, which then became the paper of Plekhanov's party, and he later started another paper for the Bolshevik party, which was called *Vperod*, meaning "Forward." For some time the Bolsheviks and Mensheviks seemed more interested in abusing one another than in trying to overthrow the Russian government, and Lenin's letters were full of angry criticism.

On December 30, 1903, for example, Lenin wrote from Geneva to the Central Committee in Russia:

> We have received your letter of the 10th December. We are astounded and indignant at your silence on fighting questions and the irregularity of your correspondence. It is quite impossible to conduct affairs in this way! Find another Secretary if the Bear [Lenin's sister, Maria] and the Deer [G. M. Krzhizhanovsky] are not able to write each week. Just imagine, up to now we have had nothing detailed from the Deer!
>
> There is so far no answer (some twenty days) to our letter of the 10th December. Such a disgraceful state of affairs must be stopped at all costs.

Lenin never lost sight of his goal—revolution. Axelrod, although he had quarreled with Lenin, wrote of him: "There is no other man who is absorbed by the revolution twenty-four hours a day, who has no other thoughts but the thought of revolution, and who, even when he sleeps, dreams of nothing but the revolution."

5

The Revolution of 1905

★

While the revolutionaries living outside Russia were quarreling among themselves, affairs in Russia were making revolution more and more likely.

In 1891, a priest living near Kazan wrote a letter which appeared in newspapers about the near-starvation suffered by the peasants around him. For one or two years there were bad harvests and this happened again before 1900, so that in some parts of Russia there was almost a famine.

Conditions might have been better if the system of cultivating the land had been different. Since the liberation of the serfs in 1861, land had been divided up among the peasants on a strip system, whereby a man held a certain piece of ground for a few years, after which there was a reshuffle, and someone else in the village took the strip while the original owner was given another.

This was fair in that, although the quality of the land varied, no one man had a very good or a very bad piece for a long time. It did not result in good farming, however, because nobody wanted to put a lot of hard work into a piece of land that would not belong to him for very long.

Often the many holidays the Russian peasants had for saints' days were largely spent in drinking, which affected the next day's work. The productivity of land in Russia was low compared with that of Germany or England.

The policy of the government during the 1890's was not fair to the peasants, since the Czar's Finance Minister, Count Sergei Yulyewich Witte, was much more interested in expanding Russia's foreign exports than in improving the life of the peasants.

Anxious to build up a gold reserve, Witte would export as much grain to other countries as he could, even when this grain was badly needed in Russia. He also wanted to please the industrial workers by keeping bread as cheap as possible, and to do this the price paid to the peasants for their corn had to be kept low. At the same time imported goods, such as sugar and tea, were expensive because of the high duty put on them, so the peasants' standard of living was poor.

Much sympathy was felt for the peasants by many of the intellectual and better-off classes in Russia, and a number of people made efforts to help them. In 1897, some of the more violent thinkers started the Socialist Revolutionary party. Unlike Lenin's party—the Socialist Democratic party, which concerned itself mainly with the workers in industry—the Socialist Revolutionaries were chiefly interested in the peasants. Their ultimate aim was the nationalization of all the big privately owned estates, an aim for which they were willing to use violent methods if necessary.

All his life Witte was very interested in railways, and, in 1891, work was begun on the great Trans-Siberian Railway, which was eventually to link Moscow with Vladivostok, on the Pacific coast. A full week's continuous traveling would be needed to make the trip. Between 1891 and 1905 nearly 20,000 miles of new railway lines were built in Russia, and at the same time industry increased enormously, especially the textile industry and the production of coal and pig iron.

As already mentioned, many of the Russian industries were managed by the English, Scots, or Welsh, such as John Hughes, who supervised coal mining in the Donets Basin from 1869.

Industry in Russia was concentrated into a few very big concerns employing thousands of people. There were practically no small factories. This great concentration enabled revolutionary agitators to work successfully, and strikes were more serious than if industry had been more scattered.

One such concern was the Morosov cotton mill, not far from Moscow, where not less than 15,000 people were employed. The Morosov family, who owned this and three or four other mills, had become extremely wealthy. They interested themselves largely in the arts. It was Morosov money that mostly paid for the Moscow Arts Theater when it was started, and one of the family made an admirable collection of French pictures, especially works by Matisse and Gauguin. But the management of the mill was left chiefly to an English family called Charnock from Lancashire.

The workers at the Orechovo mill were the population of a

small town in themselves, with their own schools, hospital, and theater. The Charnock family, worried by the revolutionary talk, especially among the younger men, introduced soccer in an attempt to divert their attention, this game being previously unknown in Russia. There were difficulties at first, but the Russians took to it, and soon there were a number of teams in Russia, on one of which Khrushchev played. At that time he was a miner in the Ukraine. No one could have guessed that after the death of Stalin in 1953, he would become virtually the ruler of Russia until he fell from power in 1964. One soccer team has become famous outside Russia—the Dynamo team. The mothers of the players at Orechovo did not like their sons to appear in shorts, as they thought this immodest, but they got used to it in time.

Although the Morosov family did not take much interest in improving the actual working conditions at their factory, one of them was a keen supporter of the revolutionary movement. He contributed a large sum of money every month to its funds and Lenin himself was later to have access to generous bequests.

Strikes and acts of violence were a perpetual nightmare to the Czar's advisers and to industrialists in Russia. Lenin, in Switzerland, eagerly read all the news that came to him from his native country, wondering when the time would be ripe for the revolution on which he had set his heart.

In 1901, a student called Karpovich murdered the Minister of Education, and a year later the Minister of the Interior, who was in charge of the police force, was shot. In 1904, the Prime Minister, von Plehve, was killed by a bomb, and in 1905, the Grand Duke Sergei, a member of the Imperial family, was killed by Kalyaev.

For some years the Czar and his advisers had been interested in developing the eastern parts of Russia. They anticipated Khrushchev in realizing what riches lay in Siberia, and decided to encourage people to go to live there and not to use it merely as a place of exile.

The city of Vladivostok, on the Pacific coast, is actually farther from Moscow to the east than is New York, across Europe and the Atlantic Ocean, to the west. Much of this vast Russian territory is very rich indeed in minerals, timber, fish, and furs. Farther south, in central Asia, near the city of Tashkent, cotton was grown, which helped to supply the mills in European Russia.

Until the building of railroads these lands were utterly remote from the western parts of Russia, and Witte was sensible in attaching great importance to the building of the Trans-Siberian Railway, which he hoped would be followed by others in central Asia.

There was considerable conflict over gaining permission to build part of the line through the Chinese territory of Manchuria, and Japanese opposition to the Russian policies led to the outbreak of war in February, 1904. The Japanese did not declare war upon Russia; they simply destroyed the Russian ships at Port Arthur, just as years later, in 1941, they attacked the American ships at Pearl Harbor, again without declaring war.

It was very difficult for the Russian commander to transport men and supplies because the railway, the cause of the war, had not been completed. The war proved very unpopular, and after the Russian fleet had been completely defeated by the Japanese off the island of Tsushima, peace was made in September, 1905.

While the war was still going on, revolution, in a very mild form, broke out in Russia. The country was becoming more and more insistent that there must be some form of elected national assembly. Czar Nicholas II, who had succeeded Alexander III in 1894, refused to grant such requests. Although promising to make some reforms, he rejected the advice of the local councils who asked for more liberties for the people, equal civil rights for all, and freedom of education. Many men, including doctors, lawyers, professors, and journalists, organized themselves into unions supporting such a program.

Port Arthur was besieged by the Japanese for eight months and fell in January, 1905.

Soon after this a sinister thing occurred. Every year, at the time of the Epiphany—the Russian calendar was later than the English one—the Czar carried out a ceremony of "blessing the water" of the River Neva at St. Petersburg. A gun salute was fired afterward from the fortress of Peter and Paul, which faces the Winter Palace. This year one of the saluting guns had a real charge in it, which did not do much damage; but the Czar did not live again in the Winter Palace.

Later that same month a body of working people marched to the Winter Palace to ask the Czar to improve the conditons under which they lived. There was nothing at all fierce about this group of people, who looked upon the Czar not merely as an autocrat but also as their "little father," to whom they could appeal for help. Some of them carried icons —religious pictures, which are greatly venerated by Orthodox Christians—and some even had portraits of the Czar.

The leader of the party was a priest, Father Gapon, who had taken a great interest in working-class conditions for some time. He was largely responsible for the founding of a society of industrial workers in St. Petersburg which provided tea-room clubs aiming to encourage a healthy national spirit, a high standard of moral conduct, and social conscience in citizens. The clubs ran various cultural activities, studied general affairs, and provided mutual aid, such as meals, when necessary.

There seemed to be some mystery about Father Gapon; his concern for the workers appeared genuine, but he was suspected by some revolutionaries of having connections with the police. Before heading the procession to the Winter Palace, he had written a very respectful statement to the Czar about the wishes of the workers.

The Czar was not at the Winter Palace, and, disastrously, the government leaders ordered troops to stop the procession, which was done by shooting at those taking part as they walked, singing religious or patriotic songs. Many were killed. The survivors turned into fierce haters of the government.

News of this reached Lenin and Krupskaya in Switzerland, and they were greatly excited, wondering if the time were near for them to return to Russia to lead a full-scale revolution.

Soon afterward Father Gapon himself arrived in Switzerland. He had been wounded while with the procession, but had escaped to the home of Gorki, the writer. He then wrote to the Czar in a very different way from his former respectful manner: "The innocent blood of workers, their wives and children lies forever between you, the soul-murderer, and the Russian people."

Gapon then fled the country. He raised funds abroad to buy arms for the Russian workers, but the English ship carrying them foundered and blew up. Gapon himself died by hanging in Finland. It was not known who was responsible for his death. His body, in a little wooden house, was not found for a month.

Lenin was even more excited by the news which reached him in the summer of that year of a mutiny on board the battleship *Potemkin* on the Black Sea. The crew managed to spread terror in Odessa and the neighborhood for some time. Lenin, for once showing little sense of reality, sent quite a young man, Mikhail Vasilyev, to the Crimea to lead the sailors, and to capture as much of the Black Sea coast and as many ships as possible, before Lenin himself should arrive. The *Potemkin*, however, had to take refuge in Rumania.

Strikes broke out continually throughout the year, and by the end of the summer the Czar had promised to call a national assembly, the Duma. Russia, in fact, would have some kind of parliament.

6

Years of Waiting

★

L enin was impatient to be on the spot in Russia to encourage the sparks of revolution which seemed about
to flare up into a blaze. It was frustrating for him to
remain in Switzerland with Krupskaya, while Trotsky, one
of the most prominent of the Menshevik party, and in a sense
Lenin's rival, had managed to return to Russia in February,
1905. Later in the year Trotsky was elected President of the
St. Petersburg Workers' Soviet.

Lenin wrote to Plekhanov, urging him to return to Russia,
without success. Lenin himself was delayed by the difficulty
of obtaining a false passport. He was much too well known
to the police as a dangerous revolutionary to be allowed into
Russia at this time under his own name, and it was not until

October, 1905, that he managed to get to Russia, using a passport made out in the name of an Englishman, William Frey.

He was held up for two weeks in Sweden in the course of his journey, waiting for the arrival of the man who was to meet him with this false passport. Once in Russia, he had to remain in hiding. He would go from place to place, spending a few days in one and then moving to another where there was somebody willing to take him in. Krupskaya followed him to Russia, but they frequently had to live in different houses.

Much happened in Russia during the autumn of 1905. The government issued what was known as the October Manifesto, stating what it proposed to do in the way of meeting demands for reform.

It was one thing to promise that there would be a Duma, or elected parliament, but how effective this would be depended upon how its representatives were to be elected, and how much power would be given to them when they were.

The Czar wanted to keep power as much as possible in his own hands. In fact, it looked as if the Duma would have so little real voice in the conduct of affairs that many of the more extreme revolutionaries, including Lenin himself, wanted nothing to do with it.

A new party had come into prominence in Russia. It was known as the Constitutional Democrats, or the Cadets. Its members were largely professional men or lesser landed proprietors who wanted to introduce a type of government based upon the English system, with ministers chosen from an elected government.

While Czar and his advisers were trying to make as few

concessions as possible, a new series of strikes occurred in Russia. At times these strikes almost brought everything in the country to a standstill: railways, industries, public services—everything was affected.

A naval mutiny broke out in Kronstadt in the autumn, and another at Sebastopol, on the Black Sea, at the end of November. The leader of the latter was a Lieutenant Schmidt, and, before he assembled the men he sent a telegram to the Czar, expressing his loyalty, and asking that a Constituent Assembly, the Duma, be called. No answer was sent to this telegram, and, when the mutiny had been put down, Lieutenant Schmidt was shot.

By the end of the year Lenin had found it advisable to go over the frontier from Russia into Finland. He remained close to the border, at Kuokkala, so that a messenger could bring letters and reports of what was happening, and take back articles written by Lenin for printing on the secret presses. Krupskaya was with him, as well as her mother and his sister Maria. Krupskaya crossed the border into Russia every day for her work and the door of their house was left unlocked at night. Bedding, bread and milk were in the living room, ready for any messenger who might come.

Lenin was in Finland when, at the end of December, a regiment of the Moscow garrison mutinied. This mutiny was suppressed.

Elections for the Duma were carried out, though not on a very fair basis, and the first Duma assembled in May, 1906. It did not have a long life, for the Czar dissolved it after only two months. It was announced that the second assembly would be in March of the following year; but so angry were the Duma members at the dissolution that almost half of them crossed the border to Vyborg in Finland, and, meeting there, passed a resolution urging the Russian people to refuse to pay taxes or to supply recruits for the army until the Duma met again.

Nothing much came of this resolution, but the strikes went on. Witte had been dismissed from his post in the government, and the next Minister of any note was Stolypin, a man who was anxious to proceed with a policy of land reform.

While Lenin was in St. Petersburg, at the end of 1905, he wrote articles for a revolutionary paper, called *Novaya Zhizn*, which means "New Life." This paper was founded by a woman called Maria Andreyevna, who was the mistress of Maxim Gorki, the writer. Gorki's real name was Aleksey Maksimovich Peshkov. Having grown up under very poor conditions, he had great sympathy with the revolutionaries, and the name he adopted, "Gorki," means "bitter."

While Lenin was writing for *Novaya Zhizn* he met a woman named Elizabeth, who had divorced her husband. Although wealthy and rather fashionable, she became interested in Lenin, and even allowed him to meet his fellow conspirators in her flat in a part of St. Petersburg where the police would not expect to find plotters.

Elizabeth did not attend the meetings herself but sometimes Lenin came to see her alone. Though they became fond of one another, they had not very much in common. Elizabeth was not seriously interested in Marxism, but she quite genuinely liked art, of which Lenin knew little and cared less. He had been introduced to her as William Frey, the name on his passport, although he was also using the name Lenin to sign the articles he wrote. The editor of

Novaya Zhizn described Lenin at that time as bald, stoop-shouldered, and badly dressed, and having Mongoloid features; but his eyes and smile were remarkable.

Elizabeth was sufficiently interested in Lenin to follow him to Stockholm when he later went there. She wrote, however, "There were days when I could not tell whether he was a man or a machine." Nevertheless, after they separated they corresponded with one another in quite affectionate terms.

In due course *Novaya Zhizn* was suppressed by the police; another paper *Volya*—meaning "Wave"—appeared, and then *Proletary*. A collaborator with Lenin on *Proletary* was Bogdanov, a man who held views with which Lenin disagreed violently. Bogdanov and some others thought the ideas of Karl Marx were too materialistic, and they developed a philosophy to combine Socialism with religion.

In 1906, after the elections to the first Duma, Lenin wrote a pamphlet entitled "The Victory of the Cadets," in which he bitterly attacked the Constitutional Democrats. This party, in fact probably the most reasonable of any in Russia at the time, was hated, not only by Lenin and his extremists, but also by the Czar. The enmity between the Bolsheviks and Mensheviks continued.

In 1905, the two groups had held separate conferences, Lenin's Bolsheviks in London, and the Mensheviks in Geneva. Early in 1907 Lenin wrote a very provocative pamphlet about the Mensheviks. He had not wanted any of the Social Democrats to recognize the Duma or seek election to it; the Menshevik wing of the party had agreed with him at first, but later decided to be represented in the Duma. Lenin's attack in his pamphlet on the Mensheviks in the party was more than the Social Democrats could stand, and they insisted on his appearing before nine men to have his conduct judged.

This experience did not seem to have any lasting effect upon Lenin and his relations with his party. Later in 1907 there was a conference of the Social Democrats, this time with Bolsheviks and Mensheviks included in the same conference, which had some difficulty meeting at all. Originally the plan was that it should meet in Copenhagen, but when the authorities there objected, the conference finally took place in London.

There were 105 Bolsheviks to 97 Mensheviks, besides about 134 others. Once again violent quarrels broke out, and, as usual, Lenin showed himself to be far more ruthless and less willing to compromise than other people. Plekhanov was there, and he was in favor of an alliance with the bourgeoisie, people who were against violent methods.

Other people at the conference included Axelrod, Martov, Trotsky, and Stalin, who was not then considered at all an important member of the party.

Gorki was also present. He lived in Capri, where he had started a kind of university for exiles, run by Bogdanov. Here revolutionaries were taught what they should strive to bring about. Gorki invited Lenin to visit him and Lenin did so, but the trip was not a success. Lenin was so violent in his talk that he made himself intolerable. Evidently realizing his failure, he left Capri after only a few days.

In spite of this, Gorki declared that there was a side of Lenin he could like. As a revolutionary Lenin was almost inhuman in his attitude, but personally he could be a gentle and interesting companion. His ruthlessness prevented him from being popular among his followers, until after the Revolution when he became the hero figure.

Lenin was criticized for not attempting to stop the "expropriations," means by which the revolutionaries gained funds. They usually took the form of an armed raid upon a bank in Russia. Large sums of money were carried off in successful coups, during which people were sometimes injured. Since these attacks upon property made a very bad impression on the Russian people, they were not good as revolutionary propaganda. Lenin could, undoubtedly, have done much to discourage them, but he wanted the money they provided.

Acts of violence carried out by peasants took place quite frequently in the country, but these were of a much milder form than the "expropriations." Sometimes the peasants on a large estate would take for themselves timber or hay that they were not entitled to, and occasionally they even set fire to the owner's property.

Lenin was not very hopeful that there ever would be a successful revolution. In 1908 he decided to leave Finland and after some traveling settled in Paris with Krupskaya, her mother, and his sister Maria.

Leaving Finland had not been easy. After getting a new passport under an assumed name, Lenin got a peasant to show him the way across three miles of ice to an island where a steamer was to call. The ice proved to be so thin that Lenin and the peasant heard it cracking under their feet as they walked. This dangerous trip might well have cost him his life.

With Krupskaya he found an apartment to live in near Paris. He was furious at the system followed by the *Bibliotheque Nationale*, which made it much harder for him to get the books he wanted to read than it had been in London at the British Museum.

After living in France for a year or two, Lenin decided that he would start a kind of school for the training of underground workers, similar to the one already existing at Capri. Many revolutionaries were in exile from Russia, and Lenin often had visits from them—people he knew well, such as Martov and Zinoviev, and others more obscure.

Lenin and Krupskaya were interested in talking with them, and occasionally gave them a meal, but there was no smoking or drinking. This was very unusual indeed for Russians. Lenin noticed that these would-be revolutionaries, away from their own country, became depressed, aimless, and time-wasters. There was not enough for them to do; they were poor and often half-starved.

The "school" was started in 1911, at Longjumeau, near Paris, in rooms rented from a leather worker. Krupskaya was greatly distressed by the hard life this man led, and the long hours he worked for small pay. She and Lenin were amazed that almost his only pleasure in life was to go to church on Sunday and listen to the singing. They did not approve of this at all, although when they went for walks the Russians in their "school" enjoyed singing folk songs.

Among their visitors was a young woman called Inessa Armand, a striking person with a remarkable history. She had been born in France of a theatrical couple; her father was French and her mother Scottish. Her parents died when she was young, and two of her relatives, an aunt and a grandmother, who lived in Russia as teachers in the house of a rich manufacturer, Armand, sent for her to work as a governess.

Inessa did very well for herself. She married one of the sons of the wealthy Armand family, and had five children. They, however, did not prevent her from feeling bored; she began to travel away from home by herself, and to become interested in the revolutionary movement. She was arrested in Russia at the time of the 1905 outbreak, but her indulgent husband provided bail. She left him for his brother, with whom she went to Switzerland, where he died of tuberculosis. Later she came to Paris with two of her children. Lenin met her and was fascinated by her, and she by him. She came to live near Lenin and Krupskaya.

Lenin's interest in her lasted until her death. Krupskaya, surprisingly, did not object and even liked to be with Inessa's children. Later Krupskaya offered to divorce Lenin, but he refused. Inessa provided him with the glamour that Krupskaya lacked, but he could not do without the companionship and care that Krupskaya gave him.

One of the revolutionaries' chief difficulties was that so many among their number were police spies who reported their plans and their secret codes. Coding and decoding the letters the revolutionaries wrote to one another took a good deal of time, most of which was really wasted because police informers were so numerous that they could easily learn the secret codes.

In Russia a rather curious kind of "police socialism" had started. Nonpolitical, it was supposed to deal with disputes in industry. This was, as its name implies, not disapproved of by the police, who were suspected of introducing *agents provocateurs* among working-class groups in order to discover dangerous revolutionaries.

All the revolutionary groups both in and outside Russia were riddled with these people, and a man whom Lenin regarded as one of his most faithful colleagues, Malinovsky, proved in the end to be one of them.

He had been with Lenin at a conference of the Socialist Democratic party held in Prague in 1912. This was as stormy as, or even stormier than, preceding conferences. Many of those present, convinced that revolution was not the right thing for Russia, wanted to turn the extremists out of the party. Lenin resisted successfully, but the conference left him, as all the preceding ones had done, on the verge of a nervous breakdown.

Krupskaya nursed him as she had done before, and then she herself fell dangerously ill with goiter. It was necessary for her to have an operation in Switzerland. This operation lasted three hours, and was performed without an anaesthetic. Krupskaya suffered to some extent from goiter for the rest of her life. She and Lenin gave up their Paris home and went in June 1912 went to live in Cracow, to be nearer Russia, although by now they despaired of revolution. They were, however, accessible to revolutionaries who often crossed the border with borrowed passports. Lenin and Krupskaya still enjoyed bicycle rides and walks in the country.

7

Russia at War

★

The years immediately preceding the outbreak of World War I in 1914 were to Lenin and Krupskaya the most depressing, for they thought that the great revolution they so longed for would never take place. Of the various political parties in Russia, one or two, and in particular the Cadets, were working for sensible reforms. Lenin hated them for this very reason, because he feared that the Russian people would content themselves with moderate reforms, taking place gradually, and never break out into actual revolution.

Czar Nicholas, although he had been forced to agree to the establishment of the Duma, hated constitutional government and wanted to retain as much power as he could for

himself. He also intensely disliked the Cadets, the majority
party in the Duma.

Members of the Cadet party were anxious to bring about
a scheme by which the peasants could own their land and
pass it on to their sons. They were in favor of taking over the
big estates compulsorily, but paying the owners compensation, and allowing the peasants to buy the land with the help
of the "Peasants' Bank." More extreme than the Cadet Party
were the Social Revolutionaries, who were in favor of taking
over the estates by force, without paying compensation.

The peasants had an advocate in Piotr Arkadevich Stolypin, the Minister of the Interior, who earnestly wanted to
abolish the communal tenure of land and to have peasant
ownership. One problem to be settled was whether land
should pass on from a father to his eldest son, or whether
all the sons should share in it. Many people were in favor of
keeping the holdings as large as possible, even though this
meant that younger sons would have to find a way to earn a
living for themselves. The well-to-do peasants, or "Kulaks,"
as they were called, were one of the classes that suffered most
in the Revolution.

Stolypin had many enemies, not all of them numbered
among the revolutionaries, though presumably the revolutionaries were responsible for the outrage that took place on
August 12, 1906. Stolypin was receiving visitors at his country home when two men wearing police uniforms entered
and threw a bomb into the reception room. There was a ter-
rific explosion, the villa was destroyed, and thirty-three people were killed, including the two men who had thrown the
bomb. The injured included Stolypin's daughter and his
two-year-old son. His daughter remained crippled all her life.

After this, the Czar insisted that Stolypin and his family take up residence in the Winter Palace.

Such violence had become so common and was such a menace to the lives of prominent men in Russia that "Field Courts-Martial" were made legal. These enabled local authorities to carry out immediate sentence upon anyone who was supposed to be concerned with an outrage. Inevitably, the fact that a suspect could be condemned and executed with no time for a proper trial led to abuses. In these courts-martial, known as "Stolypin's neckties," the business of drawing up the accusation and the trial had to be done in four days.

Some of the worst criminals escaped. A man called Kano, who lived in the Caucasus, had the reputation of being a genius as a bank robber. His immediate superior in the revolutionary organization was Josef Djugashvili, later known as Stalin. Kano, who found it hard to disguise himself because he was cross-eyed, was imprisoned, but released after pretending to be mad. He tamed a sparrow while in prison.

In 1911, the Czar was in Kiev, and a gala performance was given at the Opera. The Czar, with one or two of his family, was in a box, and Stolypin was present, sitting in the stalls. Suddenly a man sprang up and fired at Stolypin, who, desperately wounded, turned toward the Czar's box, inclined his head, and made the sign of the Cross. He died in a hospital a few days later. There was much comment on the fact that the Czar never went to visit him in the hospital, nor showed a great deal of concern at the tragedy.

Stolypin had fallen out of favor with the Czarina, if not with the Czar himself, a little while earlier, because he had written a protest at the position occupied by Gregory Rasputin, a sinister, mysterious man from Siberia who had almost unlimited influence over the Czarina. Rasputin was responsible to a very great extent for the intense unpopularity in Russia of the Czar, and still more of the Czarina, in the last years before the Revolution.

Rasputin professed to be what was known in Russia as a "starets," that is, a kind of holy man, who is not, however, in orders, nor is exactly a monk.

Rasputin, a striking-looking person, with long, dark, untidy hair, and a dirty, unwashed body, lived, in fact, a thoroughly dissolute life, indulging himself with drink and women. He did, however, apparently possess some kind of hypnotic power, and may even have had training in its use.

Rasputin had been brought to the notice of the Czarina by a lady of the Court, and his hypnotic powers were successful in helping her son, the little Czarevich, to recover from his frequent uncontrollable bleeding brought on by hemophilia, a peculiarity found only in males but inherited through the mother.

The Czarina, although she was a German princess, was a granddaughter of Queen Victoria and had spent a good deal of her early life in England. Having strict ideas about good behavior and morality, after her marriage she tried to reform the Russian court. This made her unpopular; and she was also a narrow-minded, obstinate woman, who imposed her will upon her weak-willed husband, Nicholas. Their marriage was, privately, a happy one, but to Russia the Czarina was a disaster.

She had four daughters before the longed-for son and heir, Alexis, was born. It was a cruel blow to find that he had hemophilia, from which he might die at any time. The slightest cut could produce a fatal amount of bleeding. Rasputin, with his powers of healing, seemed like a gift from heaven to the Czarina, and she, who had been so strict with the court ladies over their morals, refused to believe anything she heard of Rasputin's extremely immoral life. To the indignation of the Russians, she also took his advice upon matters not connected with the Czarevich's health, even persuading her husband to dismiss people whom Rasputin disliked, and to appoint those he proposed.

The immoral, uneducated peasant from Siberia was, in fact, becoming the real ruler of Russia. Some people such as Stolypin, made protests to the Czar, who was persuaded by his wife to pay no heed to them.

Strikes still occurred fairly often in Russia, and there was a tragic ending to one in 1912, at the Lena goldfields. For some reason soldiers who were called out to keep order fired upon the strikers, killing large numbers of them.

An organization known as "The Black Hundreds" existed to hunt out revolutionaries, with the connivance of the police. There were also frequent outbreaks against the Jews. On the other hand, steps were taken to make primary education universal throughout Russia, and it was hoped that, by 1922, this would be achieved.

Stolypin's land policy had been a step forward; but since he was devoted to the idea of Russian nationalism, he had no sympathy with the desires of the many minority nations included in the Russian Empire, such as those in the Caucasus and the Uzbeks and Turkamans from central Asia.

It was World War I that was the final cause of the Russian Revolution. For some years Russia and Austria had been rivals in influencing the Balkan states, and Austria annexed

burg, at Tannenberg, in East Prussia, with very heavy losses. This was not because the Russian soldiers lacked courage, but unlike the Germans, they were not well equipped, and they lacked good officers. They had, however, helped the French and British by drawing German troops away from the western front, thus making it possible for the Germans to be checked in their advance into France on the Marne.

The Czar had appointed his uncle, the Grand Duke Nicholas, to be commander-in-chief of the Russian armies, and, on the more southerly front, in Galicia, the Russians had a great deal of success. This was partly because the Austrians, whom they were fighting, were not such tough soldiers as the Germans. Also in that region a large proportion of the population were Slavic—Czechs, Slovaks, or Poles—many of whom had more sympathy for the Russians than for the Austrians. The Poles, although they did not as a rule like the Russians, hoped to get self-government after the war.

By the time that fighting was halted for the winter of 1914–1915, the Russians were well on their way to capturing the fortress of Przemysl, and the Austrians had lost more men that the Russians had at Tannenburg.

Things looked even better in the spring of 1915. The Russians captured Przemysl, together with a great number of men and guns. Also, the pressure on their armies was relieved to some extent by the landing of British and French troops at Gallipoli, and the entry of Italy into the war on the side of Russia and her allies. The Germans had to spare some troops to help the Austrians fight the Italians, and the Turks fight the British and French.

Unfortunately, the Gallipoli venture failed, and by the late summer of 1915 the Russians were suffering heavy losses on the Austrian front. The German-Austrian forces were able to advance all the way to Warsaw, which fell to them in August, 1915.

The Czar then made a great mistake. He removed his uncle, the Grand Duke Nicholas, from command of the Russian army and took this duty upon himself. In so doing he was acting against the advice of almost all his ministers. The person who wanted him to assume command was the Czarina, who was jealous of the great popularity of the Grand Duke with the Russian soldiers.

The Czar had no qualifications whatsoever for taking command of an army, and his ministers warned him that if the Russians suffered defeat it would greatly add to his unpopularity.

The Czar, and still more the Czarina, were fantastically obstinate; the letters they wrote to one another while the Czar was at the front reveal that the Czarina had no interest at all in improving social conditions in Russia. Her one aim was to keep the autocracy of the Czar and not yield to the ever-increasing demand for more democratic government. The Czarina wanted her delicate son to inherit absolute power. She wrote to her husband: "Be the Emperor, be Peter the Great, Ivan the Terrible, Emperor Paul—crush them all under you. . . . We have been placed by God on the throne, and we must keep it firm and give it over to our son untouched. I kiss you, caress you, love you, long for you, can't sleep without you, bless you."

The Czar, who himself admitted in his letters to his wife that he had no strength of will, obeyed her suggestions that certain ministers should be dismissed because she—or rather Rasputin—disliked them.

Few people at this time helped Lenin's cause more than did Rasputin. Before the war Lenin had practically despaired of revolution; the war made it far more likely, and Rasputin made it inevitable. The Czarina herself was extremely unpopular with the Russians, who called her "the German woman," and Rasputin used her as a tool to dismiss and appoint men to posts of authority as he wished.

Inevitably, Russia suffered very much from the war. When it broke out there was no proper organization for switching industry to the production of war supplies, for rationing goods to civilians, and for transporting men and materiels.

The defeats in the summer of 1915, with the retreat on the Austrian front, meant that crowds of refugees streamed back into Russia, leaving a "scorched earth" behind them; and all these people had to be fed. The Russian farms were without young men to work them, and the women and old men who were left were discouraged from producing much more food than they needed for themselves because there was so little they could buy with money. This meant that it was hard to find food for factory workers in towns, and already in 1915 there were food riots.

By the beginning of 1917, fifteen million men had been mobilized for military service. In fact, thirty-six percent of the country's manpower was withdrawn; half the industrial workers by then were women, and the output was only two-thirds of the normal.

In the summer of 1916 the French appealed to the Russians to launch an offensive in order to relieve the German pressure on their front at Verdun.

The Russian general, Aleksey Alekseyevich Brusilov, advanced with some success into Galicia, but the Russians had no confidence in their government. They felt their men were being killed and wounded to no purpose. A General Krymov reported to the Duma leaders that the army would welcome a *coup d'état,* and the Czar's brother-in-law, the Grand Duke Alexander, warned: "Disaffection is spreading very fast. Strange as it may seem, it is the government which is preparing the revolution."

In November, 1916, Professor Pavel Nikolayevich Milyukov in the Duma called attention to "dark forces" in government circles. Charging the Czarina and Rasputin with leading the nation into chaos, he asked after every point, "Is this stupidity or is it treason?"

In December, 1916, Prince Felix Yusupov took drastic action. He invited Rasputin to his house, and there, with the assistance of the Grand Duke Dmitri and a member of the Duma, V. M. Purishkevich, plied him with wine and cakes. Some of the cakes were poisoned, but as they were of different colors, the conspirators knew which to avoid. The poison had no effect upon Rasputin, and his hosts, beginning to think they were dealing with the Devil himself, tried to shoot him. Rasputin ran from the house with bullets in his body, but Purishkevich killed him in the snow-covered courtyard.

The police recovered his body from under the ice of the River Neva where it had been hidden, and the Czar returned from the front for the funeral. Rasputin had prophesied that the Imperial dynasty would not long survive his death.

8

Lenin Returns to Russia

★

The Russian Revolution of 1917 ranks as one of the great events in the world's history. In the development of civilization it is as important as the French Revolution of 1789 and the fall of Constantinople to the Turks in 1453.

It is, then, the more surprising that it should have begun in a very casual, haphazard way—a riot of women tired of waiting in a bread line. Even those who were most anxious that it should take place had no plans for carrying it out, any more than those who were opposed to it had any plans to defeat it. The murder of Rasputin was the only definite step taken to attempt to prevent it. Neither Lenin in Switzerland on the one hand, nor the Czar in Russia on the other, expected the revolution to come when it did.

Alexander Kerensky, a member of the Duma, who played a very prominent part in the first months of the revolution, declared only two days before it broke out that he did not expect it, although the British and French ambassadors were very apprehensive.

In January, 1917, just a few weeks before the revolution began and three months before his own return to Russia in an attempt to lead it, Lenin had written: "We, the old ones, may never live to see the decisive battles of the coming revolution."

In contrast to this, he had written in October, 1908, "The Socialist Revolution is looming in Great Britain—this only blind people could fail to see."

Earlier in that same year he had made a speech in Geneva at a gathering to commemorate the twenty-fifth anniversary of the death of Karl Marx, and he then criticized the Paris Commune for not having been more drastic in its actions during the revolt in Paris after Prussia defeated France in 1871. Lenin said in his speech that the Commune's first mistake was that the banks were not seized; the second was "the excess magnanimity of the proletariat; it should have exterminated its enemies, but it attempted to use moral influence on them."

Lenin's qualifications for leading the Russian Revolution were that he was more ruthless and more completely and calmly dedicated than anyone else. To his work for revolution he subordinated his private life and his private pleasures. Like a great many Russians he had been an avid and very good chess player, but he gave this up, because of the demand it made on his time and thoughts.

A young Russian Jewish girl, Maria Essen, who lived for a time with Lenin and Krupskaya in Switzerland, wrote an account of an expedition made by the three of them. The excursion began by a visit to the rather grim-looking Castle of Chillon at Montreux, on Lake Geneva. It was a beautiful day, and, having seen the castle, Lenin and Maria decided to climb a mountain—leaving Krupskaya, who was not equal to anything so strenuous, in a hotel.

Maria described the climb, which was quite a stiff one, and how she went up part of the way on her hands and knees. Upon reaching the snow-covered summit, Maria looked in rapture at the glorious view around and below her of lake and mountains. Lenin also looked at the view and then remarked: "The Mensheviks do make a mess of things!" Never was the cause to which he had dedicated himself out of his thoughts.

He had, however, not merely no plans for starting the revolution but, when it had broken out, he became full of wild schemes for world revolution, just as, after the 1905 outbreak, he had planned to send a quite young and inexperienced man to lead mutineering sailors to capture the Crimea.

In Russia itself dissatisfaction with the Czar and Czarina and weariness of the war were increasing as the winter of 1916–1917 drew toward spring. Before the war the surplus labor from the villages had been available for the factories, but with most able-bodied men at the front there was not sufficient labor for either farms or industries.

A young officer, who had been wounded in the war and decorated for heroism, wrote to his father, the President of the Duma: "We are ready to die for Russia, for our Mother country, but not for the caprice of the generals."

In accounts of events in Russia it is often confusing that

apparently the same event, described by different writers, is assigned two different dates, about two weeks apart. This is because the Russian calendar differed by thirteen days from that of the rest of Europe. The Russian Revolution may therefore be said by one writer to have started at the end of February, 1917, while another will put it on March 8.

On this day the Russian Revolution began when a long line of hungry people, half numbed by cold, waiting to buy bread in Petrograd, rioted because they believed that there was a supply of bread which they were not allowed to have. The rioting became so serious that troops were called out. Unlike the previous disastrous occasions when harmless people had been killed in front of the Winter Palace and at the Lena goldfields, this time the soldiers not only did not harm the demonstrators but presently were taking part in the disorders themselves. Many police, who had come in an effort to establish order, were killed either by soldiers or civilians. Petrograd was soon in a state of complete upheaval.

Strikes broke out at fifty or more factories. When news of the disturbances reached the Czar at the front he issued an Imperial Edict to dismiss the Duma. This was disregarded, and instead the Duma appointed a Provisional Committee, under the Presidency of M. V. Rodzyanko. It was decided that the Czar must abdicate, but at first it was suggested that he should do so in favor of his younger brother, Prince Michael.

Prince Michael was, understandably, very dubious about taking over the Imperial throne, and within a matter of hours the plan had been changed. The Romanov dynasty should reign no more; Russia would no longer be ruled by a Czar.

The change had taken place with great rapidity: on March

12, four days after the rioting started, Rodzyanko telegraphed
the Czar: "The last hour has come when the destiny of the
country and the dynasty is being decided." This was the
second telegram he had sent to Nicholas, the first one having
urged him to appoint quickly a Prime Minister the people
could trust. Without answering, Nicholas sent off a small
force under General N. Y. Ivanov to put down the revolution. This little army could not even reach Petrograd.

The Czar himself set out for his capital, but the line was
blocked. He went to Pskov, the headquarters of one of his
generals, where he was visited by two delegates of the Provisional Government. On March 15 he agreed to abdicate.
This he did in a very dignified way, appealing to the country
to support the new government and to go on to victory in
the war.

The Czar seemed to face the complete upheaval in his
fortunes with almost unbelievable calm. Only a matter of
days before he had refused to make perfectly reasonable
changes toward a less autocratic government, but he did
not protest at his own dismissal. He remarked, "I shall take
up dominoes again in my spare time." He and his family
were put under arrest.

There were now virtually two governments in Russia. One,
recognized by Russia's allies, Great Britain, France, and
the United States, was known as the Provisional Government. The Prime Minister was Prince George Lvov, and the
Minister of Justice, and most prominent member of the
Provisional Government, Kerensky.

There was also, working more or less in conjunction with
it, the Soviet of Soldiers and Workers, a kind of general
revolutionary committee under the Presidency of a Georgian
called Chkheidze.

The Provisional Government intended to carry on with the war, but discipline in the army was very much relaxed, and the soldiers were anxious to hurry home to secure as much land for themselves as they could. Those who were actually in the front line of the fighting rarely deserted, however.

Local government was completely disorganized in Russia, as the Provincial Governors, who had been appointed by the Czar, ceased to have any authority after he abdicated.

Lenin and Krupskaya heard the news of the revolution in Switzerland a day or two after the bread riots had broken out. Naturally they, and all the other Russian emigrés in Switzerland, were greatly excited and eager to get back to Russia.

Lenin was completely out of sympathy with such men as Kerensky and Prince Lvov. The revolution as it took place in March, 1917, hardly counted to him as a revolution at all. He hoped, however, that it might be a preliminary to the complete revolution he wanted so much.

During the first few weeks after the March revolution, Lenin expressed his views in four letters, which were later published as *Letters from Afar*. In his excited state he wrote some very unwise things, although they were no doubt what he genuinely felt. He wrote of the need for world revolution. Instead of war between Germany and the Allies, he said, the real war was between the working people and the capitalists.

In the first *Letter from Afar*, dated March 7, 1917, he wrote: "The first revolution engendered by the imperialistic world war has broken out. The first revolution, but certainly not the last.

"Judging by the scanty information available in Switzerland, the first stage of this first revolution, namely, of the

Russian revolution of 1st March, 1917, has ended. This first stage of our revolution will certainly not be the last."

Such outbursts inevitably heightened the fear that people in other countries had of the Russian Bolshevik party. After Lenin and his party had achieved power in Russia their many difficulties were greatly increased by the mistrust of the rest of the world.

The urgent problem of Lenin, Krupskaya, Zinoviev, and the other Russian revolutionaries in Switzerland was how they could return to Russia. Those who had been in exile in Siberia, such as Kamenev, Martov, and Stalin, were quickly on the spot in Petrograd; Trotsky was in Canada and did not get back to Russia for a few weeks.

Lenin turned over various schemes in his mind—such as pretending to be a Swede in order to secure a Swedish passport. This plan was not likely to be a success as he did not speak any Swedish at all. He also considered impersonating a Russian called Karpinsky—who looked after the Russian library at Geneva—and traveling to England and then to Russia.

This would mean that Karpinsky would have to be persuaded to disappear for a time, by going to some quiet spot in the mountains, but it would not be easy for Lenin to make himself look anything like him. Eventually the problem was solved with the help of the Germans. It had for some time been their policy to encourage revolution in Russia, with the hope that Russia would then drop out of the war. Since Lenin had loudly declared himself against the war, he seemed just the person to fan the revolutionary flame into something fiercer than it already was.

The Germans were prepared to arrange for Lenin and one

other person to travel secretly across Germany to Russia, but this offer Lenin refused, not having enough confidence in the Germans. He thought that, if his journey were secret, he would be at their mercy. If they decided to kill or arrest him he would be without protection.

The Germans were, in fact, sincerely anxious to get Lenin into Russia, and in the end they allowed a "sealed train" to travel across Germany with Lenin, Krupskaya, and other Russians on board.

The party of about thirty people, including Inessa Armand and at least one child, left Zürich in April.

Lenin had insisted that he and his party have no contact with Germans as they crossed the country because he feared that he might be accused of being a German agent. It was a long and rather sinister journey, but eventually the Russians, tired and travel-stained, reached Stockholm.

Lenin did not know what reception he would receive in Petrograd. As a person he was little known in Russia, although many of his articles had been published and widely read.

In Stockholm he was advised to get some new clothes before going farther. This he did not want to do, but he yielded as far as to buy shoes and trousers, and even to discard his old hat for a new one.

Meanwhile a friend of Lenin's, Shlyapnikov, arranged that he have a great reception when he arrived at Petrograd, with naval and military guards of honor.

Lenin traveled from Stockholm across Finland, and at a Russian frontier station, Belo Ostrov, was joined by a party including a woman, Alexandra Kollontai, who gave Lenin a bouquet of red roses, and Kamenev, who was then the editor of the newspaper, *Pravda*. Lenin at once began to abuse him because of the policy of the paper, which he did not like.

The train slowly steamed into the Finland station at Petrograd. Here were not only the formal guards of honor with officers who expected Lenin to inspect them, but great crowds of people who had stood waiting for hours to see him arrive and who wanted to seize him and carry him on their shoulders. Searchlights from the Fortress of Peter and Paul were directed on the scene, and Lenin was taken to the waiting room that had been for the Czar's use only, for a formal reception.

Not all the revolutionary leaders were enthusiastic about Lenin. One of them, George Tsereteli, had refused to make the official speech of welcome to Lenin. This duty was taken on by N. S. Chkheidze, the President of the Petrograd Soviet, who, since he had just been ill, and his son had died, looked very unhappy as he spoke.

"Comrade Lenin," he said, "in the name of the Petrograd Soviet of Workers and Soldiers' Deputies and the whole revolution we welcome you to Russia . . . but we believe that the principal task of the revolutionary democracy at present is to defend our revolution from every kind of attack both from within and from without. We believe that what is needed is not disunity but the closing of the ranks of the entire democracy. We hope you will pursue these aims together with us."

Lenin, in March, 1916, had written several times criticizing Chkheidze severely, and urging the need to break away from his ideas. His reply to Chkheidze's speech was not very reassuring. He said, "Dear Comrades, soldiers, sailors, and workers; I am happy to greet in your persons the victorious

Russian revolution; I greet you as the vanguard of the world proletarian army. The predatory imperialist war is the beginning of a civil war all over Europe. The hour is not far off when . . . the people will turn their weapons against the capitalist exploiters. The sun of the world socialist revolution has already risen. In Germany there is a seething ferment. Any day now we shall see the collapse of European imperialism. The Russian revolution you have made has prepared the way and opened a new epoch. Long live the world socialist revolution!"

After these speeches Lenin was taken through the shouting, cheering crowds to a house which had belonged to a famous ballerina, Kshesinskaya, a former favorite of the Czar. This house was used as a kind of headquarters. Lenin appeared on the balcony at intervals and spoke to the crowds outside.

The next day he showed a more human side of his character. He found time to visit his mother's grave in the Volkov cemetery. She had died on July 25, 1916. Lenin might well honor her memory; she had done her very best for him, interceding with those in authority when he was arrested, and supplying him with money to live on. She had loved him dearly, and Lenin's letters to her show that he loved her and was really concerned for her welfare.

"Darling Mother," he had written, in a typical letter, "I kiss you and send you my best wishes. What is the spring like on the Volga? Are you all well? . . . The other day I again went for a bicycle ride into the forest. All the fruit trees in the garden are in white blossom (as though milk had been poured over them). . . ."

9

Lenin Finds the Way Difficult

★

After they arrived in Petrograd, Lenin and Krupskaya spent the night in the apartment of his sister Anna and her husband Mark. Maria, the unmarried sister, was also there. She and her doctor brother Dmitri, had in the course of their lives been imprisoned as revolutionaries, and so had Anna's husband. Lenin, abroad when this had happened, had written them letters of good advice as to how to keep well in prison, urging them to take regular exercise in the cell, be very careful about their diet, and to keep themselves occupied with serious and varied reading: "I remember that in the evening after a meal I used regularly to read fiction for relaxation, and I never enjoyed it more than when I was in prison. Above all, do not forget the daily compulsory physical exercises. Force yourself to make several dozen different movements (without stopping). It is most important."

Lenin was not to be allowed any time to settle down with his family and rest when he was back in Russia. The very next morning he was scheduled to speak at a meeting of the Bolshevik party held in the Tauride Palace, but nobody had warned him of this. Consequently, not only had he no speech prepared, but, tired from traveling and the exciting events of the day before, he slept late and had to get ready in great haste when messengers came to get him.

On the way Lenin wrote down some notes of what he intended to say, announcing the changes he wanted to make in Russia as soon as he had power. These included the nationalization of the banks and the lightening of discipline in the army. When he made his speech to the assembled Bolsheviks in a room of the Tauride Palace, however, he entirely failed to convince his hearers. He had gone too fast for them; they were not prepared to be as drastic as he was.

The Bolsheviks became angry and protesting, and the Mensheviks were even more upset. After holding a meeting in another room of the same building, they had joined the Bolsheviks to hear what Lenin's plans were.

His popularity of the day before was short-lived. Already word was going around that he was a German agent, sent into Russia to weaken or end the war effort against Germany. Tired as the Russians were of the war, they were still patriotic, and indignant at the idea of being dictated to by a German messenger. The members of the guard of honor who had been assembled when Lenin arrived, and the officer commanding them, recorded their regret at having taken part in his reception. Within a few hours Lenin's position changed from that of a popular hero to that of a man under grave suspicion.

Lenin was undaunted. He set himself to work to build up the Bolshevik party and to get the individual members of it accustomed to his ideas. By the beginning of May, when there was a conference of the Bolshevik party, he was gaining influence.

The Provisional Government was neither strong nor very wise. Prince Lvov, the Prime Minister, was over-shadowed by Kerensky, who had become War Minister, and who was, in fact, the most energetic and capable member of the government. No Bolsheviks were included, but there were two Mensheviks, Tsereteli and Chernov.

The latter wrote an interesting comment on Lenin: "Lenin is a man of great capacities, but the abnormal conditions of underground life have dwarfed and stunted them most gruesomely. Lenin could say of himself, 'I know not where I am going, but I am going there with determination.'"

In June the "First Congress of Soviets" met in Petrograd. It was a vast affair. Over a thousand people assembled, including Social Revolutionaries, Mensheviks, and Bolsheviks. Kerensky and Lenin spoke. A Russian who heard Lenin speak remarked, long afterward, that it was when Lenin made a speech—sometimes lasting two hours—that his greatness and force of character were revealed. As a writer he was apt to be dull, but never as a speaker.

Since the March revolution there had been no police on the streets in Petrograd. In the provinces organized local government had come to an end, and even the good work of the Zemtvos practically ceased.

The Soviet of Soldiers and Workers continued to work more or less alongside the Provisional Government, which came in for a great deal of criticism for its failure to accomplish what was expected of it.

Lenin made plans to overthrow the Provisional Government by force, and the date fixed for this was July 16. A body of soldiers, assisted by sailors and workmen, attempted to seize the main buildings in Petrograd.

This was an action planned entirely by the Bolshevik party. Although the Soviet of Soldiers and Workers was by no means in perfect sympathy with the Provisional Government it was against any attempt by the Bolsheviks to take control, and Chkheidze, the President of the Soviet, had stopped one or two previous efforts to overthrow the government.

The people who came out on the side of the Bolsheviks on July 16 were largely factory workers, but a great number of sailors came by the River Neva from the naval base at Kronstadt. They succeeded in capturing the Peter and Paul fortress.

The revolt, however, was put down astonishingly quickly, largely because the soldiers of the Preobrazhensky regiment remained loyal to the government, but also because the uprising had not been carefully planned. It was a haphazard affair; many people were eager to turn against the government and even to take up arms, but there was no leadership.

Although Kerensky was away at the front when the revolt happened, the next day, July 17, the disorders were suppressed. An order was out to arrest Lenin. The Kshesinskaya Palace, which had been his headquarters, was taken over, and the sailors were turned out of the Peter and Paul fortress.

The office of Lenin's newspaper, *Pravda*, was searched; Lenin had left it only half an hour before. He became a fugitive in Petrograd, calling himself Konstantin Ivanov.

Lenin was now no longer an influential leader. He and his party had tried, all through the summer, to turn the minds of the Russian people against the war, while Kerensky did his best to fan patriotic fervor for continuing to fight the Germans. Lenin had drawn to himself a large following, especially from among the factory workers, but now, as he slipped into first one hiding place and then another—one was a watchman's hut in the Renault factory, another the house of a man called Alliluyev, whose daughter later married Stalin—he began to realize that his own party was turning against him.

It was he who was responsible for the uprising in July; this had failed, and now, where was he? He had not been killed or arrested, but he had disappeared; he was no longer guiding his party. Rumors that he was a German agent started afresh, and these were strengthened by the fact that the uprising in Petrograd had practically coincided with a German offensive at the front. This may well have been purely accidental, but it was easy to cast suspicion on Lenin who had, after all, been brought back to Russia with the help of the Germans, and was now said to have been taken away on a German submarine.

When Lenin realized the general state of feeling in his own party he considered giving himself up to the authorities and standing trial.

He did at one moment, while in Alliluyev's house, actually make up his mind to surrender, and he said good-bye to Krupskaya. People who still supported him, however, would not let him give himself up until they had negotiated with the authorities as to the kind of treatment he would receive. Because they were not satisfied about this, Lenin decided to remain in hiding.

With Zinoviev he reached a place not very far from the Finnish frontier, where he was hidden in a hayloft. Disguising himself as best he could by shaving off his beard, Lenin continued his work for the revolution. Messengers from Petrograd brought him newspapers and letters, and also took back articles he had written for circulation there.

Since the hayloft was not a particularly safe hiding place, Lenin and Zinoviev moved a little way off to a clearing in a forest on the banks of a lake. Here they lived an open-air kind of existence, eating fish caught in the lake, but still receiving the papers brought out to them and sending back messages. Lenin had started to write a book called *The State and Revolution*, in which he developed startling ideas of how the state should eventually practically cease to exist and the human community carry on its affairs without the discipline and organization the state provides.

In summer the place by the lake was quite pleasant. However, because autumn began early in those northerly regions, by the middle of August Lenin and Zinoviev wanted to find somewhere more suitable for living in the colder weather.

The best plan seemed to be for them to go over the border to Finland, where Lenin had lived before, but the difficulty was how to get there. There was train service between Petrograd and Helsinki, and one of the engineers on this line was Hugo Yalava, a Finn who sympathized with the revolutionaries. Yalava had, in fact, taken part in the 1905 revolution. He was willing to get Zinoviev, Lenin, and some other travelers onto the train when it stopped at a station that was within walking distance of where they were living. This stop was made in the middle of the night.

Unfortunately, Emelianov, the man who was to guide Lenin and Zinoviev to the train station, lost his way and they with Shotman, a secret courier, and Eino Rahja, a friend of Yalava, had a long and rather dangerous walk. Evading a forest fire, they eventually reached the station much later than planned. Then Shotman and Emelianov were arrested by station guards, who were suspicious of what they were doing. Shotman's papers were in order; he was forced to travel on a train going not to Finland but to Petrograd. Lenin and Zinoviev, also managed to board this train secretly, but got off before it reached Petrograd and went into hiding for the rest of the night at a small place called Udelnaya. Emelianov had given the guards as much trouble as he could when they questioned him, so as to gain time for Lenin, Zinoviev and Eino Rahja. He lived in the district.

Because Zinoviev did not attempt to go to Finland, it was only Lenin who needed to board the train for Finland secretly. Eino Rahja had his own identity papers in good order and could travel openly.

After waiting for the train at the place agreed upon, Lenin got on board in the darkness of the night. He traveled in the locomotive where he occupied himself with stoking the wood-burning engine. The dangerous time came when the frontier station of Belo Ostrov was reached, and every traveler's papers were examined. Hugo Yalava drove the engine, with Lenin still on board, to a siding to get water, and did not return until it was just time for the train to start off again so that Lenin would escape attention.

In Finland, Lenin stayed in a small village on the coast called Yalkala. Here he made an effort to take up country pursuits, gathering mushrooms just as he had when he was a boy in the woods at Simbirsk. He found plowing, however, too strenuous.

Lenin presently decided that he would prefer to stay in Helsinki and that it would be safer for him to do so. He wanted to receive communications almost every day from the Bolsheviks in Petrograd and to send messages out to them. It was easier to do this in a city than in a village where everyone's actions were noticed.

Besides Eino Rahja, there were other sympathizers with Lenin in Finland. When he made his way to Helsinki by stages, he stayed in the houses of people who his supporters knew would be willing to have him. In Helsinki he stayed in the home of the Chief of Police himself, a man called Gustav Rovio, who had an apartment many stories up and in the middle of Helsinki. Since Rovio's wife was away, Lenin established himself in the apartment, read the letters and papers sent him from Petrograd, and wrote. He was comfortable, but he longed to start another revolutionary coup in Russia that would put himself and his Bolsheviks in power. Leaving Rovio's flat in Helsinki on September 30, he went with Eino Rahja to Vyborg, which was close to the Russian frontier. There he lived with a journalist whose name was Latukk.

To Lenin's indignation, the Central Committee of his party forbade him to return to Petrograd. They declared that they did this for his own safety, but Lenin on October 12 resigned from the Central Committee. While he was at Vyborg, where he stayed three weeks, Lenin was visited by

Shotman, who described Lenin's fury with the Central Committee. Shotman was astonished that Lenin had no misgivings about the ability of untrained people, such as himself, to organize the machinery of Government, including finance. Lenin instructed Shotman to arrange for him to return to Petrograd. This Shotman was able to do. The Central Committee permitted his return and, disguised, he stayed in Petrograd in the apartment of Marguerite Fofanova, a woman who worked in a publisher's office. Her children were sent to stay with relatives.

Lenin, while he was in Vyborg, had begun to write a pamphlet that was called "Can the Bolsheviks Retain State Power?" This was in some respects a modification of the views he expressed in the book he had been writing, *The State and Revolution*, in which he had suggested that the state would become almost powerless. In his new piece of writing he described a state organized not so differently from what actually was done after he obtained power. Owners of estates and factories were to be dispossessed, and everyone compelled to work in order to live.

This pamphlet includes a paragraph which hints at Lenin's weak point as a leader; "As for bread, I, who had never been in need, never gave it a thought. Bread to me appeared of itself, being a sort of by-product of a writer's work. Fundamentally, my ideas upon the class struggle for bread were reached by political analysis."

Meanwhile, in Russia, the Provisional Government was going through a very difficult time. Even though the Bolshevik uprising in July had been suppressed, it had weakened the position of the government. The Prime Minister, Prince Lvov, had resigned and his place was taken by Kerensky, who was also Minister for War and the Navy. He had his hands full. He still tried to carry on with the war against Germany, in spite of the longing for peace felt by the people. At the same time the Ukraine was demanding its own government.

A vast State Conference, held in Moscow on August 25, was attended by 2,500 people, representing various interests: the army, the civil service, the Church, and landowners. Ever since the July uprising the government had turned more toward the left, but there were many people who disapproved of this and who had counterrevolutionary views. Some of these people thought that Kerensky was not forceful enough; they wanted to have a leader with a strong personality who could lead the country away from the Bolsheviks.

A possible leader seemed to be General Lavr Kornilov. He decided to march upon Petrograd and take possession of it with his troops. Kerensky naturally was alarmed, realizing that the general probably intended to supplant Kerensky and make himself a military dictator.

Kerensky had the railway tracks removed from around Petrograd so that Kornilov's army could not reach the capital easily. His soldiers included what was known as the "Wild Division." This consisted of men from the Caucasus, mostly Moslems who were unable to speak Russian. In spite of this they managed to fraternize with Kerensky's troops, whom they were supposed to overpower. Kornilov's attempt failed. He and General Anton Denikin, who was backing him, were arrested, and another supporter, Krymov, committed suicide.

Kerensky's position was still not a happy one. The Social Democrats held a conference at the end of September, at which Kamenev proposed a resolution of lack of confidence in the Provisional Government and in its power to defend Petrograd from the Germans.

On October 20, Kerensky and the Provisional Government finally dissolved the Duma. It had had a life of eleven years, started as a result of the revolution in 1905, and now ended as a result of the 1917 revolution.

10

The October Revolution

★

One of the results of Kornilov's unsuccessful effort was that the Bolshevik party increased in numbers and influence, in spite of the fact that Lenin himself was out of Russia until October 20.

The Presidium, or governing body, of the Petrograd Soviet, resigned on September 19. In the elections which then followed Trotsky succeeded Chkheidze as Chairman, and was in fact, for a week or two, a more important person than Lenin himself in directing the coming revolution.

The Bolshevik party had been increased by some recruits from the Mensheviks, who felt that their own party was becoming too conservative, and others from the Social Revolutionary party, who were dissatisfied because this had now split into two, a right and a left wing.

The Provisional Government was still trying to carry on the war against Germany, although Lenin declared that Kerensky would surrender Petrograd to the Germans. The Bolsheviks now had a majority in the Petrograd Soviet and also in the Moscow one. Their headquarters in Petrograd was the Smolny Institute, formerly a school for girls of noble families.

On October 23 a meeting was held at which the Bolsheviks decided to launch a revolution against the Provisional Government by violent means—in fact, to make another attempt to do what they had failed to do at the end of July. The meeting had been called by Lenin himself, but was organized by Sverdlov, and held in the apartment of a man called Sukhanov, who was away. His wife, however, provided tea and sandwiches. Seven men were elected to serve as a "Politburo," Lenin, Trotsky, Stalin, Kamenev, Zinoviev, Bubnov and Sokolnikov. The decision to embark upon revolution was made despite the fact that two of the chief members of the Bolshevik party, Zinoviev and Kamenev were against it, and had made a protest in a newspaper run by Gorki.

The revolution, however, could not now be stopped; on October 29, the Petrograd Soviet established a Military Revolution Committee, under the chairmanship of Trotsky. He had a most remarkable gift for oratory, and in this way he managed to swing the garrison of the Peter and Paul fortress in Petrograd to the support of the Bolsheviks on November 5.

Trotsky, in fact, carried out the revolutionary *coup* in Petrograd with great efficiency and very little bloodshed, although fighting went on for about a week in Moscow.

Lenin was still in hiding. Lodgings had been found for him in a house on the outskirts of Petrograd, but all he could do there was write, and he fretted at what he considered Trotsky's slowness.

Kerensky, feeling that the Bolsheviks were on the point of trying to overthrow the Provisional Government, cut off the telephone to the Smolny Institute on November 5, and he also had the offices of the Bolshevik newspaper, *Rabochy Put*, seized, much of the equipment destroyed, and thousands of copies of the paper burned. The editor of the paper at this time was Stalin. Kerensky's men sealed up the office when they left, but the Bolsheviks were able to break it open again.

Trotsky laid in provisions at the Smolny Institute to be in readiness for a siege if necessary. If routed from the Institute, he planned to retreat to the Peter and Paul fortress. Kamenev suggested that if they were driven from the fortress, they should then go on board the cruiser *Aurora*.

Trotsky's well-made plans did not miscarry. The October Revolution, as it is called, is considered to have started with some shots fired from the cruiser *Aurora*, berthed on the Neva River at Petrograd.

Orders from the Provisional Government that the *Aurora* was to leave her moorings, were disobeyed, and the crew took part in the uprising on the side of the Bolsheviks. This fact caught the imagination of the revolutionaries, and the *Aurora*, still berthed on the Neva, is pointed out to all visitors to Leningrad, as Petrograd is now called.

Trotsky managed to secure the railway and telegraph offices practically without bloodshed. Kerensky's government leaders were in the Winter Palace and the only troops who attempted to defend them were a women's battalion and some young officers in training.

Kerensky, deciding to take advantage of a car which the American Embassy put at his disposal, escaped to organize resistance to the Bolsheviks outside Petrograd.

Eventually Kerensky made his home in the United States, where he outlived by many years not only Lenin, but also Trotsky and Stalin.

After the departure of Kerensky, resistance in the Winter Palace more or less collapsed. The ministers of the Provisional Government were formally put under arrest by a not very ferocious looking person, wearing a pince-nez and a broad-brimmed hat, called Antunov Obseyenko. He had fallen into a puddle on his way to the Winter Palace and his clothes were covered in mud, making him even less impressive than usual.

Marguerite Fofanova, the woman in whose house Lenin was living in hiding, brought word to him that the bridges in the city were being closed by orders of Kerensky. Lenin, realizing that he was in danger of being completely cut off from the headquarters of his party, became even more impatient and frustrated. He could not rest, and on·the morning of November 7, unable to bear the knowledge that he was away from the center of events, he took the great risk of making his way to the Smolny Institute in the center of Petrograd, over a bridge that was still open.

To lessen the danger he disguised himself by putting on a wig and tying a bandage around his face as if he had a terrible toothache. After reaching the Smolny Institute safely, he was at first not recognized by his friends there. Once recognized, however, he took control and made up for his period of inactivity by the furious energy he threw into everything he did.

By November 8 the Bolsheviks had practically won the day and Lenin could use the power he had wanted for so long. Even then few people, if any, seem to have realized how lasting the Bolshevik seizure of power was to be. Lenin himself appears to have expected to remain in charge for a few weeks only, and on November 8 the newspaper, *Izvestia* (News), wrote: "The Bolshevik uprising is a mad adventure. . . . We are quite confident that the Bolsheviks cannot organize a State Government."

The two most urgent matters were the ending of the war with Germany and the question of the land. With regard to the latter, Lenin practically adopted the policy of the Social Revolutionaries by issuing a decree abolishing private ownership on anything but a very small scale.

Lenin appointed Trotsky to look after Foreign Affairs, but he preferred to change the word "minister" in the Bolshevik government to "commissar." Lenin took the title "President of the Soviet People's Commissars." Krupskaya, who had not gone to Finland with Lenin, was now with him again.

Tiflis in the Caucasus and Kiev in the Ukraine established their own self-governing regimes; the Cossacks of the Don were against the Bolsheviks, and the Petrograd Revolutionary Government knew that the Germans might at any time advance upon the city, which also had to defend itself from any troops Kerensky had persuaded to fight against the Bolsheviks.

There were 480 Cossacks under the command of a General Krasnov, who was prepared to march with them against Tsarskoye Selo, a summer palace of the Czar a little way out-

side Petrograd. This was garrisoned by 16,000 soldiers, and
there were about 200,000 in Petrograd itself. General Krasnov declared that to march with such a small force would
ordinarily be absurd, but that in civil war things were different, for then resolution was everything. He said he well knew
the habits of the Petrograd garrison, who stayed up late
drinking and were hard to wake in the morning.

He proposed to take Tsarskoye Selo at dawn and trust to
the effect of this upon the morale of the Petrograd garrison,
who might then come over to his side.

He did, in fact, succeed in taking Tsarskoye Selo, but on
November 13 he proposed a cessation of hostilities.

The British Ambassador in Petrograd at this time, Sir
George Buchanan, was surprised by the calm of the city.
He reported that on November 7, "though a certain amount
of firing went on during the day, the Bolsheviks practically
met with no resistance, as the government had neglected to
organize any force for their own protection. In the afternoon
I walked down the quay to the Winter Palace Square and
watched from a distance the troops surrounding one of the
government buildings, whose evacuation had been de-
manded." Sir George described Lenin quite simply as an
anarchist.

The French Ambassador was more elaborate in his de-
scription of Lenin, saying he was an Utopian dreamer and a
fanatic, with no idea of what was impossible or absurd. He
also accused him of having no feelings for justice or mercy
and of being full of a crazy vanity.

The American Ambassador had wired his State Depart-
ment on October 30 that he was beginning to think that
the Bolsheviks would not make a demonstration after all. He

added that he was sorry for this because he believed senti-
ment was turning against them, and if they attempted to use
force it might teach them a useful lesson.

A foreigner in Petrograd who knew more of what Lenin
really thought than the ambassadors did was the *Manchester
Guardian's* Russian correspondent, Arthur Ransome, who
was on quite friendly terms with Lenin. He later wrote
Swallows and Amazons and other stories for children.

In spite of the war and the revolution some artistic life
still went on in Petrograd. Karsavina, the leading ballerina,
danced, and Chaliapin, the great singer and actor, appeared
in opera.

Russia was in danger—from the Germans with whom they
were still fighting, as well as from their own government.
Lenin and his Bolsheviks now had more power in the land
than any other party, but they were quite without experience
of how to govern and organize. There was a great deal to
criticize about the civil service and the administration of
Russia in the days before the Revolution, but there were
then in office some men, at least, who knew how their jobs
should be done. Once in power the Bolsheviks had to decide
matters concerning the war, finance, and agriculture with no
experience whatsoever. For instance, a man called Pestkovsky
wanted to find a minor job for himself, but after he had said
that he had studied banking at London University, he found
himself appointed, with Lenin's approval, to be the Director
of the State Bank.

On November 18 the first snow of the winter fell in Petrograd and transformed the whole scene from gray, depressing
mud to a sparkling whiteness, above which gleamed the
golden domes of churches.

Immediately after the Revolution a great number of people—over a thousand in fact—assembled in Petrograd for a full Congress of Soviets. Kamenev was elected to be Chairman of the Assembly, which included not only members of the Bolshevik party, but also Mensheviks and Social Revolutionaries. One of the first acts of the Congress was to abolish the death penalty, and this made Lenin angry, although it was a move very much in accordance with his former views. He said, however, that it was impossible to conduct a revolution without having the power of sentencing people to death.

Lenin was determined that the Bolshevik party should be the absolute rulers, although Kamenev wanted them to share power with the Mensheviks and the Social Revolutionaries, pointing out with good reason that if only one party ruled there would be terror. The leaders of the Revolution at this time were far from being in agreement with one another. Stalin, now prominent in the Bolshevik party, did not agree with Lenin that socialism in Russia must fail unless capitalism were overthrown in the West.

Lenin himself, who in fact did not know a great deal about the people in Russia because he had lived abroad so long, energetically threw himself into the organization of defense, keeping as his main object the quick conclusion of a peace with Germany on the lines of neither side's gaining territory from the other. He was determined to do this independently of Russia's wartime allies: England, France, and the United States.

The Russian soldiers, realizing that land was to be given to the peasants, were desperately anxious to hurry home and secure their share.

Lenin's headquarters were still in the Smolny Institute with its long corridors, and he and Trotsky felt that they would have liked roller skates to go from one room to another.

Gorki, the writer, was in sympathy with the Revolution, but mistrusted Lenin and his handling of it, accusing him of "experimenting with the blood of the working classes." On November 21 Gorki wrote in his newspaper that the working man should know that under Lenin he would have to face hunger, the complete disorganization of industry, and prolonged anarchy.

"Lenin," Gorki wrote, "possesses a quite exceptional strength of character, complete lack of morality, and an aristocrat's contempt for the masses. It does not worry Lenin that Russia must suffer this tragedy. He does not know the masses, he has never lived with them; he has learned from books how to make them revolt."

It was Lenin's utter ruthlessness and his single-minded devotion to the idea of revolution in Russia which won and maintained power for the Bolsheviks. He was not interested in power for himself for a selfish reason, but because he did not think that anyone but himself could carry through the Revolution, and in this he was almost certainly right.

11

Lenin as Supreme Ruler

★

Although Russia was in an extremely dangerous and difficult position in the autumn of 1917, after the October Revolution, Lenin did not seem troubled by any doubts about his own capability of dealing with the situation.

No one yet had made the experiment of trying to run a country on the theories laid down by Karl Marx. Lenin, who had hitherto been only a writer and occasionally a speaker on the ideal socialist state, now found himself often changing his viewpoint in order to meet the situation of the moment.

It is almost impossible to state Lenin's aims clearly, because details of them, and very important details, changed, but he remained entirely sure that the Bolshevik party—presently known more usually as the Communist party—must rule Russia on a non-party system, and that he must be the dictator of it. He also aimed at world communist revolution. Here, however, his ideas were not quite as clear-cut, for he had been most insistent, especially before the Russian Revolution actually took place, on the rights of every race to self-government. The Poles and the Ukrainians, for instance, should be free of Russia, the Irish of England, Nice of France—in fact, the map of Europe should be full of small, independent countries.

On the other hand, he advocated a great uprising of the proletariat in every country, which was to be above all feelings of nationality, and which would represent the hitherto oppressed social classes all over the world—classes that would in the future rule over their former rulers. This second point of view was, no doubt, the one that Lenin really felt, but he probably thought that to champion the rights of small nationalities governed by great powers was a way of promoting revolutionary feeling.

One of the few people from the West with whom Lenin talked much at this time was an American, Colonel Raymond Robins, who was in Russia as the head of the American Red Cross there. Colonel Robins himself was quite a character. He had been at one time a miner for gold and later a social worker in Chicago. His life had been saved by a vision, guiding him when he was lost in the snow, and he was a devout Christian. Lenin seems to have liked him, though when they talked they disagreed with one another.

Lenin accused the American government of living in the past, and he told Colonel Robins that the real power at the present time was economic, and that he intended to govern Russia by representatives of the important industries of the various regions. Thus the representative from Baku, in the Caucasus, would be someone concerned with oil; from the Donets Basin, someone expert in coal mining; from the great cornfields of the Ukraine, a farmer; and so on.

Much had been written and said by Lenin about the coming elections for a Constituent Assembly to represent the whole of Russia. In *Pravda* on November 19, Lenin wrote, "Comrade Workers! Remember that you yourselves now govern the State. No one will help you unless you unite and take all the affairs of the State into your hands. Your Soviets are organs of power, organs with deciding voices and full powers to act."

The elections for the Constituent Assembly, which took place on November 25, were not entirely favorable to Lenin. His Bolshevik party had a majority in Petrograd and Moscow, but over the country as a whole they did not win a clear victory over the other parties, the Left Social Revolutionaries being very strong in the country districts. This was not surprising, because the Bolsheviks had concerned themselves with factory workers rather than land workers, whereas the chief interest of the Social Revolutionaries was to secure the land for the peasants.

Lenin, although he was determined not to work in any kind of coalition with the Social Revolutionaries, nonetheless practically took over their policy for distributing the estates to peasants when he drew up his manifesto on the night following the October Revolution. He also declared that the banks, the mines, railways, and factories were to be run by the state. The result of the November elections might seem to put an end to Lenin's intention of ruling Russia by a Bolshevik dictatorship. Lenin, however, was not going to let his plan, which he regarded as absolutely necessary for carrying on the Revolution, be upset by the result of an election.

It gave him, nevertheless, a new and difficult problem to add to that of the war and the lack of food in the country. He was dedicated not only to the idea of the Revolution—*that* he had already achieved—but to the rule of himself and his chosen Bolsheviks after the Revolution. He had intended to show this to be the wish of the mass of the Russian peasants and workers. Now elections had been held all over the country that had not given him the absolute power he wanted.

Lenin faced this troublesome problem in a ruthless way. Since it was necessary that he should have absolute power, and since the Constituent Assembly had not given it to him, the Constituent Assembly must go.

By December, 1917, the newly elected members of the Assembly were making their way from distant parts of Russia toward Petrograd in readiness for the opening session.

Difficulties were put in their way for traveling, and several deputies belonging either to the Social Revolutionary or the Cadet party were arrested before the Assembly met. Not satisfied with this, the Bolsheviks outlawed the Cadet party, so that no one who professed to belong to it could sit in the Assembly. Two members of the party were actually murdered by some sailors and soldiers while lying in bed in a hospital in January 1918, just before the Assembly was to open.

Lenin had dissolved the Military Revolution Committee,

but replaced it with something far more sinister known as the Cheka. This was an organization of secret police, whose duties were not to seek for criminals of the usual kind, but to arrest people suspected of being against the Bolshevik government. The Cheka were responsible for a great deal of misery and injustice. They were eager to show themselves active and to make arrests, and the fact that their work was carried on in secret made it easy for a person to give information against anyone he did not like. That person would then be taken away by members of the Cheka in the middle of the night and probably never seen again.

Ordinary Russian citizens, not knowing whether some chance word they had said might be taken as showing disloyalty to the government, lived in dread of a visit from the Cheka.

The Constituent Assembly met in the middle of January and was expected first of all to approve the various changes that Lenin and Trotsky had decided to make since the October Revolution. The Assembly elected as Speaker Victor Chernov, who was a right-wing Social Revolutionary. He made a speech which showed that he did not intend to let the Bolsheviks have everything their own way without dispute. Measures would be put to the vote. In a fierce debate that went on until the early hours of the morning Chernov read a decree nationalizing land, and another urging that Russia and her allies make peace with Germany.

The Assembly, which did not break up until after four o'clock in the morning, had intended to meet again later that same day. Armed detachments prevented this, however, and it never met again.

This put an end to hopes that Russia would be governed in a way that truly represented what the people wanted. In-

stead, the government was to be led by a group of the most
extreme thinkers in the country, and anyone known to be in
disagreement with them would be in danger.

No one but Lenin would have been forceful enough to
organize this. Although the October Revolution had been
carried out more by Trotsky than by anyone else, had it not
been for Lenin the future government would almost certainly have been carried on by a kind of coalition of two or
three different parties.

Lenin must have found it hard to justify his treatment of
the Constituent Assembly even to himself. In later years he
remarked that the countryside must always follow the lead of
the cities, and both Petrograd and Moscow had given a majority to the Bolsheviks.

Gorki wrote an editorial that appeared in his newspaper,
comparing the way the Constituent Assembly had been
treated with the soldiers' firing at Father Gapon's procession.
No one but Gorki would have dared to write this.

Lenin, trying hard to make peace with Germany, sent
Trotsky, the Foreign Commissar, to negotiate with the Germans. An armistice was declared in December, 1917, while
the talks went on.

The peace that the Russians wanted to make was one in
which neither country gained land from the other or paid an
indemnity. The Germans had different ideas, and the terms
they offered were so harsh that Trotsky, eager as he was to
end the war with Germany, felt sure they could not be accepted. By the end of December he had adopted a "no
peace, no war" policy—he did not want to make peace on the
German terms, but neither was he prepared to start fighting
again.

Germany, although she made the terms so hard, wanted

to make peace, and in particular to be able to use the corn grown in the Ukraine's fertile "black earth" to feed her hungry people.

The Ukrainians had set up their own government with which Germany was anxious to conclude a treaty. Such an arrangement, of course, would not at all suit Lenin, for he would not be able to send soldiers across the Ukraine to the Caucasus, where there was fighting against the Bolsheviks led by anti-Bolsheviks known as White Russian generals, nor would he be able to use the Ukrainian corn for Russia.

Trotsky returned to Brest Litovsk at the end of January, hoping to spin out the talks with the Germans as long as possible. Although quite good at negotiations, he disliked the Germans much more than Lenin did. And in February Germany made a treaty with the Ukraine. Soon afterward the armistice with Russia was ended and the fighting began again. This put Lenin in a very difficult position. He moved the capital from Petrograd to Moscow in case Petrograd fell to the Germans, and Moscow has remained the capital ever since.

Because this move was very unpopular with the workers in Petrograd, Lenin left that city for Moscow as secretly as possible. With him on the train were Krupskaya and his unmarried sister, Maria.

In spite of his hatred of the capitalist countries, France and England, Lenin discussed with their representatives in Moscow the possibility of continuing the war against Germany.

Lenin found, however, that he must accept the German peace offer because the German armies were advancing too fast into Russia. This he did in March, although by then the

Germans had made their terms even harder than before. Russia was to lose an enormous amount of territory and also to pay a big indemnity to Germany.

In fact, this treaty of Brest Litovsk was not important because before the end of the year, 1918, Germany had been defeated by the Allies and the treaty was undone.

Russia did, however, in August of that year send Germany a large amount of gold. Lenin was glad of the opportunity which peace with Germany provided of having an embassy in Berlin. This, under the Ambassador, Yoffe, became a center for revolutionary propaganda in Germany.

Lenin, in spite of all his problems in Russia, remained faithful to his aim—a revolution of the proletariat all over Europe.

12

Civil War

★

The treaty of peace signed with Germany in March, 1918, did not mean that Lenin no longer had any fighting to do. Many in Russia were against the Bolshevik government. In fact, several generals and an admiral, with large forces under them, fought the Bolsheviks so hard in various parts of the vast Russian territories that at one time it looked as if they would be successful in defeating Lenin's government.

In addition to the anti-Bolsheviks themselves there were troops sent by Russia's allies in the war, who had various reasons for wanting to defeat the Bolsheviks. The Japanese, who in World War I fought on the same side as the English, Russians, and Americans, landed a large force at Vladivostok, on the far eastern coast of Russia. They wanted to take advantage of the general confusion in Russia to acquire a useful foothold in Manchuria for themselves. They were the most eager and persistent of all the foreign armies in Russia, and it was not until 1922 that they finally left Russian territory.

The Japanese, with some difficulty, persuaded the Americans to send a much smaller force to Vladivostok; the English sent some troops to the far north of Russia, landing at Murmansk and Archangel; and the French, English, and Italians sent a few soldiers to the south of Russia. They hoped to prevent large quantities of war materiel from falling into the hands of the Germans, and also to put down Lenin's Bolshevik, or, as it is now called, Communist, government. Lenin was not content that Russia had had a revolution and was now ruled by a Communist government. He desired, and fully expected, that revolution would soon break out in other European countries. His wish to export communism made other governments very eager to see him out of power.

In addition to the foreign soldiers sent by the Allies who cooperated more or less with the White Russians—as those who opposed the Communists were called—there was a large body of Czech soldiers who had been taken prisoner by the Russians during the war, or who had deserted from the Austrian army, but had said that they would like to go to France to fight against the Germans. Before World War I, Czechoslovakia was part of the Austro-Hungarian empire, and the Czechs, who are Slavs, wanted to be free to govern themselves. They hoped that if Germany and Austria were defeated in the war their country would be given independence. This did in fact happen, and it was arranged for these soldiers to be shipped from Archangel to France.

After the Revolution put difficulties in their way, the Czechs realized that the Russians were not going to send them to France. However, the Czechs, determined and enterprising men, decided that, if they could not leave Russia by the north, they would make their way along the Trans-Siberian Railway to Vladivostok and embark for France from there. This, of course, was an extremely long journey, but the Czechs undertook it, fighting their way along, and frequently joining forces with the White Russians.

In the course of their journey, the Czechs captured the important city of Kazan, near the Ural Mountains. With the city they captured the large gold reserve of the Russian State which had been taken to Kazan during the war because that city was farther away from the German front, and so safer than the capital.

Kazan was recaptured by the Communists later on in the Civil War, but the fate of all the gold captured by the Czechs remained a mystery. The Czechs, for a time, had control of the Trans-Siberian Railway. As a fighting force, they were better organized and more efficient than most of the Russian armies at that time.

The White leader in the north of Russia was Admiral Kolchak, a fine and able man who styled himself "Supreme Ruler of Russia." He was in contact with English forces from Archangel, and some of the Czechs were to make their way to that port and to Murmansk, leaving those who had already gone some distance toward Vladivostok to continue that long journey.

Kolchak was away on a mission to England and America during the October Revolution, and he wanted to offer his sword to the English. He was persuaded, however, to organize the White Russians in Siberia.

In the south of Russia a General Denikin was the White leader—General Kornilov was killed quite early in the Civil War—and a General Yudenich led a force that very nearly captured Petrograd.

Besides these leaders there were others, picturesque adventurers, who hardly knew what they were fighting for. Such a man was the Ukrainian, Makhno, who described himself as a Communist-Anarchist. He had an intense love for the Ukraine, and after being away from it for years in prison in Moscow, returned there to organize, very successfully, a communal life in Gulyai-Polye, where small industries were run by the peasants themselves. A Ukrainian patriot who did not want to be ruled by Great Russia, at one time in the course of the Civil War he fought for the Bolsheviks, at another time against them.

While traveling about disordered Russia he met various leaders and was interviewed by Lenin himself in Moscow. Makhno knew nothing about the theories of communism, but Lenin made a deep impression upon him. He asked Makhno many questions about the people in the remote countryside. Lenin was dismayed to find that his Communist propaganda did not reach those who lived only a short way from the railway line.

Lenin and Makhno were poles apart, although Makhno shared some of Lenin's views. Lenin liked to do things in an ordered way, whereas Makhno was a guerrilla fighter and a very good one. He was Russian in his intense love for his country; Lenin was not a lover of his country nor of people but entirely dedicated to a cause.

Makhno organized a guerrilla army, which fought General Denikin and defeated him. Many peasants would fight for Makhno who would not fight for Trotsky's Red Army, which commandeered their horses. Makhno, a hard-drinking, extremely courageous man, who wanted to do away with all authority, was very popular with the peasants, and he always found time to attend their weddings.

After Denikin was defeated and escaped from Russia, the Red Army overran Makhno's beloved Ukraine. He fought against the Bolsheviks, was defeated, and fled from Russia, destined to live the rest of his life in exile. Although Makhno had at one time greatly helped the Red Army, Lenin was furious that he had escaped.

Trotsky began his great task of building up a Red Army in January, 1918. This he did very well, using many officers who had served with the Czar's forces. A number of the former officers had thrown in their lot with one or another of the White leaders, but there were enough left to train an army for Communist Russia. Trotsky arranged that a certain number of trusted members of the Communist party should be included in every detachment of soldiers, and he also started schools for the training of Red officers.

There were, for a time, several White governments, which did not always get along well together. The two most important had capitals—one at Samara in the south, and the other at Omsk in Siberia. Had the White Russians been of one mind, they would almost certainly have defeated the Reds, but some of them, especially those in Siberia, had completely reactionary ideas; some others were members of the Constituent Assembly, under the Presidency of Chernov, which Lenin had dismissed, and they wanted a democratic government. Kornilov and Denikin came from humbler homes than either Lenin or Trotsky. Many of their supporters were from the Social Revolutionary party.

The Cossacks, groups of people living in certain parts of Russia who to some extent made their own laws, were noted as soldiers and horsemen. Wanting to rule themselves in groups under their "Atamans," they were against the Communists.

Eventually all the Whites were defeated. Probably more of the peasants would have joined them if they had offered something more definite and attractive than merely overthrowing Lenin's Communist government. The peasants did not want to go back to the conditions of Czarist Russia.

There was a terrible shortage of food in Russia after the Revolution. Much less than the normal amount had been produced while the most vigorous men were away at the front, and large parts of the country were devastated by fighting. Public services, transport, and factories were in confusion because so many of the people who understood how to run them had either been killed, had fled the country, or had joined one of the White armies. Lenin had to bring food into the cities to feed the factory workers, and in order to get this food patrols of soldiers were sent out to take it by force from the peasants.

They took so much—unless the peasants were very clever at hiding the grain—that sometimes the unfortunate farmers had to eat the corn that should have been saved for sowing the next year. It was said, "Before the Revolution the land was God's and the rye was ours; now the land is ours but the rye is God's."

Lenin and Krupskaya lived very simply themselves, although they were housed in the Kremlin, a group of palaces and cathedrals with golden domes, surrounded by a high red wall and towers, in the heart of Moscow. They had a five-room apartment: three bedrooms, a large kitchen, and a sitting room. Beyond, on the same floor, was Lenin's office. Someone who visited them and had tea with them mentioned that there was one teaspoon between two people. Lenin was never interested in having the luxuries and grand manner of life that most people who attain power enjoy. Power was to him the opportunity of doing the work he was dedicated to doing.

He worked very hard in his office, planning, studying reports, and interviewing many people; his interest remained, however, far more with the city dwellers than with the peasants.

After the peace treaty with Germany an Ambassador, Count Mirbach, came to Moscow, just as Russia sent one to Berlin. There were many Russians who hated the treaty with Germany, and, in June, 1918, Mirbach was assassinated. The assassins, a man called Blumkin and an assistant, asked for an interview with Mirbach about a supposed relative of his who had been arrested. Mirbach and two of his staff saw them. Blumkin fired at Mirbach, who was sitting at a table, and missed. Mirbach ran out of the room, followed by Blumkin, who shot him dead and then threw a bomb which severely damaged the room. In the confusion, Blumkin and his helper got away in a waiting car. Blumkin was never punished for this crime, and even had an important post later on. Instead, a number of people who were not in favor with the Communists, mostly Social Revolutionaries, were put to death as "accessories."

A bigger tragedy happened in July. The Czar and his

family were living as prisoners in a town called Ekaterinburg, now called Sverdlovsk, toward the north of Russia. A contingent of Czech soldiers, making their way toward Archangel, was known to be not very far from Ekaterinburg, and the order was given that the Czar and all his family be shot. In a tragic morning the Czar, Czarina, their four daughters, invalid son, three servants, and even pet spaniel were all killed. The reason for this was, no doubt, in order that they should not be released by the Czech army. Also, Lenin had found it difficult to know what to do with them. Five days after the former Royal family were killed, the Czechs reached Ekaterinburg.

This ruthless crime naturally made the worst possible impression abroad. The Czarina had been extremely foolish and the Czar weak, but this could not excuse the killings.

More violence was to follow. The German Commander-in-Chief in the Ukraine was assassinated in Kiev on August 1, and at the end of that month Lenin himself was nearly killed by a young woman, Dora—sometimes called Fanny—Kaplan.

Lenin spent a good deal of his time making speeches to workers. In two speeches on August 30, he drew attention to the fact that in various parts of Russia there were counter-revolutionary activities. For example, land and factories were being restored to their former owners.

As Lenin left the hall after making the second speech, Dora Kaplan, who belonged to the right wing of the Social Revolutionaries, pushed her way near to Lenin with the help of another Social Revolutionary, Novikov, and fired three shots at him, two of which hit him. He was taken home to the Kremlin, where it was found that one bullet had broken his left shoulder and the other had entered his left lung. If this bullet had been deflected by even a millimeter it would have killed him. Dora Kaplan had spent many years in prison and had poor eyesight. It was thought that this saved Lenin's life.

Dora was arrested, put in prison, and later executed.

Unfortunately, it was not only she who suffered for this attempt on Lenin's life. As a result of it the Cheka became very active in hunting out possible enemies of Lenin and the Communists, and hundreds of people were arrested and disappeared.

Lenin made a good recovery up to a point, but probably his injuries shortened his life. The doctors decided not to attempt to remove the bullets, and he lived with them in his body.

For his convalescence he and Krupskaya went to a village outside Moscow called Gorki, where there was a palatial house which had belonged to the rich textile manufacturer, Savva Morosov, at whose factory in Orechevo-Zuevo Lenin had once stayed in hiding. A few rooms of this house were used for Lenin and Krupskaya to live in. Lenin took up his boyhood occupation of looking for mushrooms in the woods, and sometimes had the pleasure of a visit from Inessa Armand. Occasionally she brought along one of her daughters, and Lenin liked talking with this young girl, who cheered him.

Meanwhile the Civil War continued, but soon after the attempt upon Lenin's life, the war began to go better for the Communists. They recaptured Kazan from the Czechs, and also Simbirsk, Lenin's birthplace. The Japanese, however, advancing from Vladivostok, set up a White Russian, Semenov, to rule in eastern Siberia under their direction.

After the defeat of Germany in November, 1918, the Allies with the exception of Japan, began to lose interest in helping the White generals in Russia. Their soldiers were eager to return home. In spite of this the White generals had nearly succeeded in defeating the Reds in the early part of 1919.

Yudenich almost took Petrograd, and, at the same time, Kolchak was fighting in the north and Denikin in the south. But by the autumn of 1919 the Reds had retaken most of the important cities they had lost. The last of the White generals to continue to fight was one of the ablest of them, General Wrangel, who succeeded Denikin in the south. He did not give up until November, 1920, after being defeated by a Communist army. Then he and many of his supporters escaped from Russia by the Black Sea and became refugees.

The end of Admiral Kolchak was tragic. A Czech detachment, trying to get out of Russia, betrayed him to the Reds. He was killed in February, 1920.

The fact that the Whites were eventually defeated was probably due more to Trotsky than to anyone else. Having taken on the task of organizing the Red Army, Trotsky watched over it devotedly, and rushed about the country to visit and encourage detachments that were having particularly hard fighting to do.

He was a most successful War Commissar. Lenin, even before he was wounded, showed little interest in traveling. He remained at work in the Kremlin.

Convalescing at Gorki in the winter of 1918–1919, he had much to worry him, apart from the Civil War that was going on. People were dying all over Russia from hunger and from epidemic diseases brought on by starvation and misery.

Lenin was bitterly disappointed that a full-scale revolution had not broken out in Germany after her defeat. He had been absolutely confident that world—or at least European—revolution was just around the corner. There had been a revolution in Germany at the end of the war, when the Kaiser was deposed, but the country had quickly stabilized itself and set up a republic that was not Communist.

In March, 1919, Bela Kun headed a Communist government in Hungary, and Bavaria had one in April of that year, but neither of these lasted very long.

Lenin was also worried during the 1918–1919 winter about Krupskaya's health. She had never really recovered from her goiter trouble and now it became worse than before. She was also tired out from caring for him during his convalescence.

He decided to send her away from the big house at Gorki to the village of Sokolniki, where she could help with the children's school. Although she had none of her own, Krupskaya adored children. Sokolniki was not too far away for Lenin to go to visit her in the evenings, which he did.

When the New Year came there was a party for the local children, and Lenin joined them in dancing around the tree. He even played a game with them, "Koshkamishka" (cat and mouse). In 1919, when summer came, Krupskaya went for a trip on the Volga River on board the *Krasnaya Zvesda* (Red Star). This was a journey organized to do propaganda work among the people who lived near the banks of the Volga.

Russia's former allies were now busy trying to settle the terms of the peace treaty with Germany. Poland was to become an entirely free country, but there was some difference of opinion as to where her boundary should lie. The Poles claimed a line which would include in their country a number of people who were not Polish. Naturally the Russians were opposed to this.

The Poles are brave fighters, and they invaded Russia in April, 1920, in the hope of establishing their claim to the land they wanted in Russian territory. They got as far as Kiev. Trotsky's Red Army then successfully drove the Poles out of Russia and pursued them into their own country. It looked as if Warsaw must fall to the Russians, who had a very promising young commander, Colonel Budyenny. He was to become a successful general in World War II.

Lenin was overjoyed by this advance into Poland. All his hopes, which had been disappointed for so long, of a Communist revolution in other countries revived. He was convinced that the Poles would welcome the Red Army as allies in the fight of the workers against the capitalists, and that in a short time the Polish revolution would be accomplished.

He did not consider the strong love of the Poles for their own country, and their hatred of the Russians which had increased in the long years when they had been a conquered nation, partly under Russian rule. When the Red Army really threatened Warsaw, the Poles made a supreme effort and drove the Russians out of their country.

By the autumn of 1920 the war with Poland was over and the Russians defeated. The Polish leader was Marshal Pilsudski, who, with his brother, had been a fellow-conspirator with Lenin's brother, Alexander, in 1886.

A deep personal grief came to Lenin in October, 1920, when Inessa Armand died of typhus during an epidemic in Russia. Lenin attended her funeral, and those who saw him there remarked how utterly stricken he looked.

13

The New Economic Policy

★

lthough, early in 1921, the White generals had been
defeated, and the Civil War was at an end, Russia
was now faced by enemies worse even than foreign
foes or their own soldiers fighting against the government.
These enemies were hunger and disease, and they claimed
millions of victims.

The terrible famine in Russia was partly caused by bad
harvests and partly by Lenin's policy of taking the food
which the peasants produced away from them by armed
bands. Although they were paid something for it, the money
was practically useless because so little was produced in the
factories that they could not spend it.

During the Civil War the various districts in Russia, under

different rulers, issued their own paper currencies, which often became valueless when there was a change of ruler.

Since nearly all that they produced was taken from them, the peasants hardly exerted themselves to produce more than they needed for themselves. Lenin and his associates found it hard to interest peasants in the new form of government. They had been ready to revolt against the Czarist regime in order to own their pieces of land and live more comfortably. When they found that the land was to belong to the state and the result of their labor taken away, they lost faith in the new regime. Even the town workers, during the days of the Civil War, were discontented, and took part in serious revolts.

Workers at the Putilov factory walked through Petrograd with banners: "Down with Lenin and horseflesh. Give us the Czar and pork."

Lenin and his co-workers in the Kremlin worked very hard indeed, Lenin especially, to find ways of getting the country on a working basis. Food rationing was introduced, and for this people were divided into different categories; those who were doing really heavy physical work received about three times as much as those who were employed in lighter industries, and four times as much as the former bourgeois class, many of whom were doing nonphysical work.

As is almost inevitable when there is severe rationing of essential goods, there was a good deal of "black marketing." People who had articles they could spare illegally exchanged them for food if they could find someone able to provide it. Most factories paid their workers partly in goods and partly in paper money.

A very troublesome problem was that of the Trade Unions, and it fell largely to Trotsky to cope with this.

During the time that fighting was going on it was thought necessary to conscript labor. People doing civilian work were put under discipline and forbidden to leave their jobs just as if they were soldiers.

The war, famine, and disease had created a great shortage of labor throughout the country. Prisoners were forced to work, and this kind of forced labor was used for many years.

The Trade Unions were inclined to think their function was to look after the interests of the workers and protect them, whereas the government wanted to use them to insure that work was done.

Propaganda was started about the merit of doing Saturday work, and those who were actually members of the Communist party were expected to make a point of working on Saturday to set a good example. Lenin, in the Kremlin, did a "Communist Saturday."

He was anxious to get the peasants to work on "collective farms" instead of on their little independent holdings, but the peasants hated this. Lenin did not like the richer peasants, who could employ others to help them; and the cultivation of land by the poorer peasants, each family with just one horse to help them, was very uneconomic. Eventually, collective farming was accepted in Russia, but every man is now given a small piece of land of his own, on which he works in his spare time.

Lenin was never afraid of adapting his policies to circumstances. The aim of his life was revolution throughout Europe, but he realized that he must lay such aims aside for a while and devote himself to stabilizing Russia, if his own government were not to crumble.

In the spring of 1921, a very serious warning came from

the sailors at the Kronstadt naval base. In 1917, the sailors had been particularly active in helping the revolutionaries, but now they were utterly disappointed with the Communist government, which they planned to overthrow by force. They advanced, wrapped in white cloaks, across the ice of the River Neva, and with the greatest courage fought the Red troops with which Trotsky opposed them.

It was a gruesome and a very bloody battle, at the end of which the sailors were defeated. Had they laid their plans more skillfully, and not allowed Trotsky to have warning of what they were going to do, it is quite possible that they might have been successful.

They had asked for liberty of press and speech, an end to the one-party government, and the right of the peasants to own cattle and to pay fixed taxes instead of having their produce taken away from them entirely.

Realizing that he must make a big change, Lenin took a step for which courage was required, as it went against his previous aims. It also made many of his Communist colleagues very angry.

This policy, introduced in April, 1921, at the time of the Kronstadt mutiny, is known as the New Economic Policy, or, more conveniently, as the N.E.P. It did, to some extent, reintroduce capitalism, and it succeeded in providing an incentive to both peasants and factory workers to produce far more than they had before.

All foreign trade remained in the hands of the state, and so did the biggest and most important factories. Other, smaller concerns were to be run by "co-operatives" of workers, but individual peasants were to be allowed to sell privately any surplus produce.

The big change for the peasants was that, instead of the government's taking everything it could from them, leaving them hardly enough to live on, they were to pay taxes of a fixed amount. What they had left over they could either use for themselves or sell privately, as they chose. They were also allowed to keep cattle and to buy extra land. This change of policy saved the country, for production went up tremendously. Lenin had to accept the criticism from some of those with him that his new policy would turn many village people into kulaks—that is, wealthy peasants.

Even the N.E.P. could not save Russia from the effects of a terrible drought which occurred in 1920–1921, and, added to the other circumstances in the country, produced a dreadful famine. This was especially bad in some areas, and with starvation came an increase of epidemics, especially typhus.

Another sad feature in the country were the many bands of "wild children," who roamed about, stealing what food they could. These boys and girls had lost their parents because of the wars, epidemics, or famine—and some because, at that time in Russia, there was a complete shedding of marriage responsibility. These homeless children were a tragic menace in Russia until in the end many of them were collected into homes, largely by the efforts of one man, and trained to earn their living.

Lenin was realistic and faced the situation. He knew that, in the long run, the food-producing peasants were the key people in Russia, even more important than the factory workers, whom he understood better. He had learned that he had to control both sectors very carefully.

In his sparsely furnished study in the Kremlin, Lenin saw a number of people, and he usually tried to do his best for them. He had only the bare essentials of office equipment round him except that on his desk was a curious ornament: a figure of a monkey playing with a skull.

"We know," he wrote, in defense of his change of policy, "that only agreement with the peasantry can save the socialist revolution in Russia, unless revolution begins in other countries. . . . Let's reconsider our policy in relation to the peasantry."

Factory production in Russia suffered tremendously from the lack of men with experience in management. Lenin preferred to be inconsistent rather than unrealistic, and he criticized the idea that the workers could run factories successfully by themselves. "Is it really true," he asked, "that every worker knows how to administer the State? Practical men know that this is a fable. We have not even liquidated illiteracy. . . . Who among the workers has done any managing?"

In fact, many of the former directors of factories were used to run them, because it was found they could not be replaced.

In 1921, Lenin's attitude toward foreign capitalist states began to change. He, who had hiterto eagerly waited for revolution throughout Europe, now found that it was essential for the well-being of Russia that she trade with other countries, even capitalist ones.

In 1919, the Third International came into being. Otherwise known as the Comintern it was an association of the Communist parties of various countries. These parties had as their object, of course, the promotion of revolution in their homelands, and the Third International met at intervals in Moscow. The discipline was very strict, and no one might attend the conference whose party loyalty was not completely vouched for by his fellows.

At the meeting held in Moscow in July, 1920, the atmosphere was full of the coming revolution in Europe, but in 1921 there was a decided change of feeling. Lenin, in March, 1921, signed a trade agreement with Great Britain, the first capitalist country to do this, though there had been an informal agreement with Sweden.

Lenin had as his Foreign Minister an able man, and a very hard worker, called Chicherin, of Italian descent. Helping with economic policy was Sokolnikov, a man who really understood business matters. He was one of those who had returned to Russia in the "sealed train."

Although the N.E.P. showed signs of improving living conditions in Russia, it could not immediately relieve the people who were dying of hunger and disease. Conditions were so terrible that Gorki sent a telegram to Herbert Hoover in America, who later became President, begging him to help. This was an amazing contrast to the previous attitude of the Communists, who could not find words bad enough for capitalists.

Herbert Hoover responded nobly to Gorki's appeal for help, and a number of people, many of them Quakers, prepared to go to Russia. Food and supplies were collected.

Lenin, at first, was unwilling to admit them, since he was convinced that they would bring not only food and clothes but also propaganda against the Communists. In the end, however, the relief organization was allowed into Russia, and it did splendid work, saving the lives of many people.

Gorki did a great deal for Russia at this time. Unlike Lenin, he had known great poverty in his childhood and youth, and he could understand and sympathize with people who were going through hard times.

Fortunately, although he was himself a writer and particularly interested in the arts, he also admired scientists, and he realized what a disaster it would be for Russia if her scientists were arrested and their work interfered with. At that time there was a Russian who was considered the greatest physiologist in the world: Ivan Petrovich Pavlov, famous for his work on nerve systems and the producing of certain kinds of behavior by stimulating reflexes.

Pavlov was already an old man when the Revolution took place, and he was a devout Christian. Lenin, an atheist, had done all he could to abolish Christianity in Russia. Days of the week were no longer called by their names, but simply by the date—the names have now been reverted to—and instead of a Sunday holiday there was a "rest day" every eight days. The majority of churches were closed.

Pavlov, however, firmly closed his laboratory on the old Sundays and went regularly to church. When brought before the dreaded Cheka for questioning he told them that he must hurry back to his laboratory to attend to an important experiment.

Fortunately Gorki had impressed upon Lenin that Pavlov must be valued, and he was, in fact, allowed to do as he chose about his religion, and Russians were very proud of him. He was a lovable and very active person even in old age.

Scientists and professors of lesser importance did not have easy lives, even if they escaped imprisonment. Those at the University of Petrograd, for instance, would from time to time be called upon, with their students, to leave their lectures and work at the docks, unloading cargo.

The idea behind this was that all classes should share in

the really heavy work—Lenin had also decreed that those in charge of forests should do tree-felling with peasants. This plan was, of course, extremely wasteful, since badly needed trained scientists gave up time to work at jobs for which they were untrained and could not do well.

If an unfortunate professor—or student—lost a button from his coat still more time would be wasted. He could not just go and buy one to replace the loss. He first had to go to a police headquarters, describe his need, and get a form authorizing him to have a new button. This form had to be taken to an office in another part of the city for a signature, and then only could the owner of the lost button go to a store to claim a new one—when he would very likely find that supplies of buttons had run out.

The writer was in Moscow on the day of Gorki's funeral in 1936—he survived Lenin by twelve years—and all activities in the city were suspended during the funeral. Countless processions walked through the streets, some formal, others just groups of men, women, and children. Portraits of Gorki mounted on poles were carried in these processions, surrounded with red or black cloth.

Gorki wanted the Revolution because he thought it would help the people of Russia have happier lives. To Lenin it did not matter so much if the Revolution brought misery; it just had to be. Unlike Gorki, he was more interested in pressing on with it than in trying to lessen the suffering. He introduced the N.E.P. to avoid disaster, not to ease unhappiness.

Not many foreigners visited Russia in the early years of the Revolution, but George Bernard Shaw and Bertrand Russell, the philosopher, did, and saw Lenin himself. They were impressed, as most people who met him were, by the force of his personality and his intellect.

Lenin had always been a great reader; he was less effective when he was dealing with matters that could not be learned entirely from books, such as science. This had not interested him until he realized how extremely useful it might be to Russia to have electrical power all over the country. Then he took up this idea with enthusiasm, and eventually electricity penetrated into even remote regions of Russia, though this took many years to achieve.

Lenin enjoyed attending to details and was particularly pleased with the State Seal he designed himself.

14

The Death of Lenin

★

Although Lenin had apparently made a good recovery from his injuries after his near-assassination, he was, early in 1922, showing signs of suffering and ill health. Since he would not spare himself in his work, it probably was a combination of overstrain and the effects of his wounds that led to his early death. He complained of violent headaches, and it was decided to perform an operation in April, 1922, to remove one of the bullets from his neck. The other one could not be removed.

The operation was successful, but in May Lenin had a stroke. He spent the summer convalescing at Gorki, but continued to work a good deal, to keep a tight hold upon Russian affairs.

Fortunately, the Commissar for Foreign Affairs, Chicherin, was an able man. Now that Russia was beginning to have relations with other countries, Chicherin had to attend various meetings outside Russia.

In April, 1922, a conference on international trade was held at Genoa, attended by representatives of most European countries, including Chicherin. England, France, and other countries insisted that Russia must pay her debts to them. At the time of the Revolution there was, in Russia, a great deal of foreign-owned property and capital, especially in factories and industry, and the new government was asked to honor these debts.

Chicherin made conditions for doing this: if Russia paid them, she must be granted full diplomatic recognition by the countries concerned, and she must also be compensated for the damage done to her by the Allied troops who took part in the Civil War.

The sum required for this was many times that of the estimated value of foreign property in Russia, and nothing came of these proposals, though Russia was, in fact, very anxious to start trade with the West and obtain credits for this purpose.

Chicherin then had a meeting at Rapallo in Italy with German representatives, with whom he succeeded in coming to an agreement. The Germans were still, as a result of World War I, no more favored by other European countries than Russia was, for a different reason, and the two nations reached an agreement with one another, part of which was for Russia to manufacture some kinds of arms and war materiel for Germany. This was kept as secret as possible. The nations which had fought and defeated Germany were, of course, very watchful lest she should start to rearm again.

Another important point to be discussed was whether the

Straits of Bosphorus should be open to ships from the navies of countries not on the Black Sea coast. A conference about this was held at Lausanne in the autumn of 1922.

England wanted the Straits to be open, but Russia was against this—most understandably, as the Russian navy was very small by comparison with the British, and if one or two English warships entered the Black Sea, they would easily be in control. The matter was not settled at the Lausanne Conference; eventually England had her way, but this was not decided until after Lenin's death.

By 1922, the Bolsheviks, or Communists, were the only political party that counted in Russia. In 1920 there were still groups of Mensheviks, who had meeting places in Moscow and other cities. Georgia, in the Caucasus, was an independent republic under Menshevik government; a number of the former Mensheviks, including Trotsky himself, had joined Lenin at the time of the Revolution; others either left Russia if they could, were arrested, or ceased to take part in public life. The last meeting in Moscow at which Mensheviks spoke publicly was at the end of 1920, and the Georgian republic later became one of the Soviet States.

It was longer before all the Social Revolutionaries had vanished, because their great strength lay in the country, and people in fairly remote villages continued to think along the lines of the Social Revolutionaries, since it was harder to reach them by propaganda. It was not until about the end of 1921 that the Social Revolutionaries ceased to be an influence in Russia.

Lenin, though he could not work as strenuously as before, was determined that Russia should no longer be a backward country. He became interested in plans for education, for promoting industry, for electrification, and for the development of Russia's vast mineral resources. Immense strides were made with these projects after his death.

The Cheka, or secret police, had been abolished—only to be replaced by another force, known as the Ogpu, which was feared just as much.

Russia had wonderful art treasures. The Imperial family, the nobility, and wealthy merchants, such as the Morosovs, had made magnificent collections of pictures, jewelry, furniture, and all sorts of *objets d'art*. The Communists, fortunately, realizing that these things must be taken care of, carefully put them into museums. Some of the beautiful houses of the nobility were taken over to be museums, and occasionally the owner was allowed to work as curator, living in perhaps one room of his former home.

Lenin spent most of the summer of 1922 recuperating in the country at Gorki. Krupskaya, although she was herself in poor health, looked after him devotedly. In the autumn Lenin returned to Moscow and made the last speeches in public that he was to deliver.

At the end of 1922 the official name of Russia became the U.S.S.R.—or, in Russian, S.S.S.R., the letters standing for "Union of Soviet Socialist Republics."

Lenin had another attack of illness, probably another stroke, in December, 1922, but his brain continued to work vigorously, and he wrote what is known as his *Testament*.

When it became evident that Lenin would not be able to continue to rule the U.S.S.R. for very much longer, the question of who should succeed him became of vital importance. The man with the strongest claim undoubtedly was Trotsky.

Through many years of exile he had worked for revolution; he organized the successful October uprising; and, thanks to his management, the Red Army was able in the end to win the Civil War.

Trotsky had a serious rival in Joseph Stalin, a Georgian who was an unusually good organizer. Joseph Djugashvili—this was his real name—was the son of a cobbler, who died while Joseph was a boy. Joseph for a time went to a seminary to train as a priest, but he gave this up and became more and more involved as a revolutionary. He was arrested more than once, and he spent some time in exile in Siberia. He was there when the Revolution first broke out.

During the years before World War I he had come to Lenin's notice. He had visited Lenin and Krupskaya while they lived at Cracow in Poland, and had written an article on Marxism which pleased Lenin very much.

After the October Revolution, Stalin became Commissar for Nationalities—that is, he was to look after the interests of the many minority races in Russia. Being a member of one of these himself, he might well have found this a suitable post, but his ambitions were far from satisfied. He was more interested in making his way up to the top position than in looking after the small nationalities.

In 1922 Lenin made him General Secretary of the Communist party, which could have been taken as an indication that he would succeed Lenin. Soon afterward, however, Lenin must have realized that Stalin was not suitable to be the supreme ruler.

Lenin wrote of him: "Comrade Stalin, having become General Secretary, has concentrated enormous power in his hands, and I am not sure that he always knows how to use that power with sufficient caution." Lenin, in fact, definitely turned against Stalin as a possible successor. Stalin probably knew this, he was not on good terms with Trotsky, and at least once was rude to Krupskaya on the telephone.

Lenin further described him: "Stalin is too rude, and this fault, entirely supportable in relations among us Communists, becomes insupportable in the office of General Secretary. Therefore I propose to the Comrades to find a way to remove Stalin from that position and appoint to it another man, who differs from Stalin only in superiority—namely more patient, more loyal, more polite, and more attentive to comrades, less capricious."

Stalin had helped to produce the newspaper *Pravda*, which was founded before the Revolution with money provided by the son of a Kazan millionaire. The paper started again in April, 1917.

Lenin had a third stroke in March, 1923. Now partly paralyzed, he could not speak, but Krupskaya patiently set to work to teach him to do this again, and during the summer and autumn in the country she had some success.

Lenin liked to have his only nephew with him—Victor, the son of his doctor brother, Dmitri. He was able to go out in a wheelchair, and both Krupskaya and his sister Maria kept him company.

In October he insisted upon being driven into Moscow, where he visited his apartment in the Kremlin and his office He was even able to walk around them. Also, he started to write again, using his left hand.

In November he received a delegation for the last time, which gave him a present of cherry trees. By the New Year it was expected that he would recover; he was at a children's party at Gorki, and saw presents being given from a tree.

Later in January, however, Lenin suddenly became worse, and on January 22, he died.

The grief of his fellow countrymen was intense. The weather was bitterly cold. With the temperature at 30 degrees below zero Fahrenheit, it was extreme even for Russia; but three-quarters of a million people passed his body as it lay in state. Some of these people had walked all day to do so; all had waited five or six hours, no small feat of endurance.

A stream of people still walks past his mummified body every day as it lies in the massive red granite tomb in the Red Square of Moscow, against the wall of the Kremlin.

Petrograd has become Leningrad in his honor.

Lenin was not greatly interested in human beings; he devoted his whole life to a cause that he believed in. He was, however, fond of his family—his mother, sisters, his brother, and nephew—and seems to have liked children, although he and Krupskaya had none. He was also fond of animals. He had a dog he loved, and once, when out hunting, refused to shoot a fox because it "looked so beautiful."

He was ruthless, and never neglected to carry out an action because of the human suffering it might involve if that action was necessary for his cause. He was not, however, cruel for personal reasons.

Although his very cool and orderly mind was in some ways more German than Russian, Lenin, when he talked, used a Russian's exaggerated expressions—"They are not men, but miserable dishrags"—and he had a Russian's idea of humor. Gorki, the writer, who often disagreed with him, said after his death that only Lenin, and no one else, could have led Russia through the Revolution. This is no doubt true, but

Lenin did not lead the Russians from an autocracy to a democratic government. He gave them a different form of autocracy. Lenin, though ruthless, tried to organize Russia on an acceptable basis, though it was a dictatorship. He died long before he had finished his task, which was taken over by the far more ruthless Stalin.

More than forty years after his death, Lenin is still the great hero of the Russian people. Neither Stalin nor Khrushchev nor anyone else has attempted to dethrone him.

BIBLIOGRAPHY

Carr, E. H., *A History of Soviet Russia*. New York, Macmillan, (Also Pelican Books, 1966.) London edition, 1950–1953.

Charques, R. D., *The Twilight of Imperial Russia*. Oxford, Oxford University Press, 1958.

Clarkson, J. D., *A History of Russia from the Ninth Century*. London, Longmans, 1962.

Fischer, Louis, *The Life of Lenin*. London, Weidenfeld & Nicolson, 1965 (also Harper & Row).

Footman, David, *The Civil War in Russia*. London, Faber, 1961 (also Praeger).

Hill, Elizabeth, and Doris Mudie, eds., *Letters of Lenin*. London, Chapman, 1937

Krupskaya, N. K., *Reminiscences of Lenin*. Trans. by B. Isaacs. Moscow, 1959. (Another version trans. by Lawrence & Wishart, London, 1930.)

Mazour, A. G., *Russia: Tsarist and Communist*. Princeton, New Jersey, Van Nostrand, 1962.

Moorehead, Alan, *The Russian Revolution*. London, Collins and Hamish Hamilton, 1958 (also Harper & Row).

Pares, Bernard, *A History of Russia*. London, Jonathan Cape, 1926. Also 1937, 1947, and 1955 (also Knopf).

Payne, Robert, *The Life and Death of Lenin*. London, W. H. Allen, 1964 and 1967 (also Simon & Schuster).

Wolfe, B. O., *Three Who Made a Revolution*. London, Thames & Hudson, 1956. (First published, New York, Dial Press, 1948.)

Index